New Heinemann Maths

Organising and Planning Guide

D1789268

Heinemann Educational Publishers
Halley Court, Jordan Hill, Oxford, OX2 8EJ
a division of Reed Educational and Professional Publishing Ltd

Heinemann is a registered trademark of Reed Educational and Professional Publishing Ltd

OXFORD   MELBOURNE   AUCKLAND
FLORENCE   PRAGUE   MADRID   ATHENS
SINGAPORE   TOKYO   SAO PAULO
CHICAGO   PORTSMOUTH (NH)   MEXICO CITY
IBADAN   GABORONE   JOHANNESBURG
KAMPALA   NAIROBI   KUALA LUMPUR

© Scottish Primary Mathematics Group 1999

Writing team

John T Blair

Ian K Clark

Percy W Farren

Archie MacCallum

Myra A Pearson

Dorothy S Simpson

John W Thayers

David K Thomson

First published 1999

04 03 02 01 00 99
10 9 8 7 6 5 4 3 2 1

ISBN 0 435 16747 2

Designed and illustrated by Gecko Limited, Bicester, Oxon.
Printed and bound in Great Britain by Ashford Colour Press, Gosport, Hants.

Acknowledgements

The objectives listed in the charts on pages 28–39 and 45 are from the National Numeracy Strategy publication *Framework for Teaching Mathematics from Reception to Year 6*, © Department for Education and Employment.

Contents

Introducing New Heinemann Maths

Mathematical development

New Heinemann Maths is a course designed to help teachers implement the content and teaching approaches described in the National Curriculum and the National Numeracy Strategy. Its clearly defined structure provides progression from Reception to Year 6 and offers schools a teaching programme with both coherence and continuity.

There is an emphasis on direct, interactive teaching aimed at helping children to develop a range of mental calculation strategies. These include the ability to recall basic facts quickly, calculate accurately with pencil and paper, use appropriate mathematical vocabulary and make connections between different areas of mathematics.

Effective teaching

Each mathematical topic in the *Teaching File* is developed systematically through a series of carefully structured lessons and linked *Pupil Activities*. The lessons provide the opportunity for direct, interactive teaching, and oral and mental work involving the whole class or a group on a daily basis.

Numerous *Pupil Activities* are provided to consolidate key teaching ideas and support group work, differentiation and discussion. Some of the small group activities require the children to work together in order to play a game or solve a problem. Suggestions on a range of simple and effective teaching resources to help motivate the children, illustrate a key teaching approach or enhance participation are included in each section of the *Teaching File*.

Classroom organisation

The components of **New Heinemann Maths** are designed for use in a flexible way. This ensures that the needs of children and teacher are met, whatever form of classroom organisation is used. Interactive *Teaching* activities can be used with a whole class or a large group. There are suitably differentiated *Pupil Activities* and written practice, consolidation, application and extension work in the *Activity Books* designed for use with groups, individuals or the whole class. These can be used to allow the teacher to work uninterrupted with any children needing additional support.

Mental calculation

The course stresses the importance of children developing the ability to 'work things out in their heads'. There is, therefore, an emphasis on oral, mental mathematics, rapid random recall of basic number facts and children explaining their methods. To acquire the necessary skills and the confidence to do this, number facts and a range of mental calculation strategies are taught and practised in a systematic way. Children are encouraged to memorise these facts and to use mental strategies when they cannot recall them.

Planning for learning

Detailed advice and examples of long- and short-term plans are given on pages 17–20 of this *Organising and Planning Guide*. The emphasis is on creating a coherent and manageable form of planning that reflects the guidance given in the National Numeracy Strategy.

Assessment and recording

New Heinemann Maths provides a range of assessment materials designed to help the teacher build up a detailed picture of the children's attainment and to check that key objectives are being met. These materials complement the teacher's ongoing informal assessments, which are carried out on a daily basis by interacting with children or observing them at work.

The assessment material may cover a short section of work in a *Check-up*, or a whole topic in the assessment pages of an *Activity Book*, or provide an end-of-year *Round-up* where different areas of mathematics are assessed. The materials can be used as part of the process of giving feedback to children and remind them of the progress they have made. They also provide a comprehensive record of achievement that can be shared with parents and other teachers.

Involving parents

Home Activities can be used to support a school's commitment of actively involving parents in their child's learning. They provide a number of straightforward activities that give parents confidence in helping their child with mathematics. For the child, *Home Activities* provide opportunities for further practice and consolidation.

2 New Heinemann Maths components

NHM 1 consists of the following components.

For teachers: *Organising and Planning Guide*
Teaching File
Teachers' Resource Pack

For children: *Activity Books*
Check-ups (including *Round-up* tests)
Pupil Sheets (included in the *Teaching File*)
Home Activities (included in the *Teaching File*).

Organising and Planning Guide

- The guide outlines:
  - the main features of the course
  - the component parts of **NHM 1**
  - relationships to the National Numeracy Strategy.

- It provides advice about:
  - planning to use the course effectively
  - organising resources
  - teaching lessons and follow-up work
  - assessing learning.

- Also included are:
  - charts to show the mathematical content of **NHM R**, **NHM 1** and **NHM 2**
  - a mapping to the key objectives of the National Numeracy Strategy in a framework planner and topic planner for the year
  - an example of a weekly planner
  - pupil record charts
  - an assessment record grid
  - a class record sheet for the key objectives.

Teaching File

- The file contains:
  - a bank of *Starters and other mental activities* to supplement those included in lessons throughout the file
  - teaching notes giving suggestions for lessons, pupil activities, further teaching, the use of the *Activity Book* pages, follow-up activities and assessment
  - photocopiable *Pupil Sheets* for use either within a lesson or as follow-up practice, consolidation or extension
  - photocopiable *Home Activities* to give homework linked to the work in school.

Starters and other mental activities

- The *Teaching File* has a bank of 23 suggestions for oral mental activities. These are intended to promote a 'feel' for number, quick recall of number facts and the flexible use of mental calculation strategies. They are designed to be interactive, involving the teacher and the whole class, or a large group.

- Used as 'starters' at the beginning of lessons, the activities help to keep skills 'ticking over', even when the main teaching has moved to another topic. They can, however, be used at any time for practice or consolidation, as well as to check whether children are ready for the next step.

- Some of the activities are *generic*, providing a 'format' which can be adapted to suit different topics. The remainder are linked to *specific* topics. This activity is used for 'Addition facts to 10'.

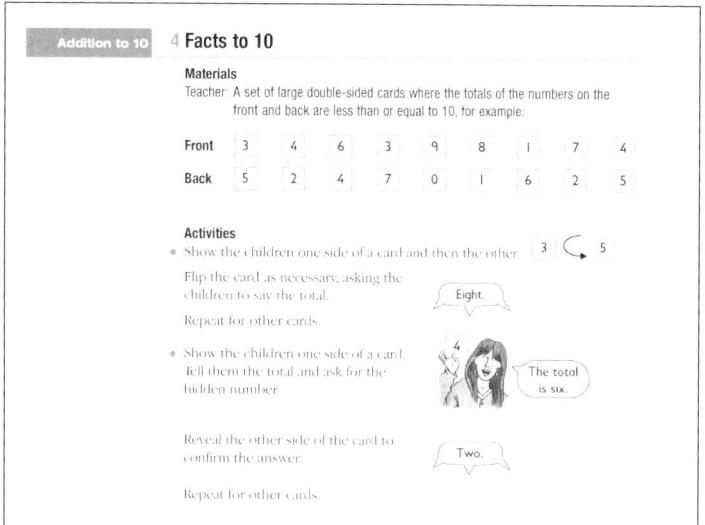

Teaching notes

- **NHM 1** includes the following mathematical topics:

Numbers to 20	Money	Length	Time
Addition to 10	3D Shape	Weight	Data Handling
Subtraction to 10	2D Shape	Capacity	

- At the beginning of each topic a summary page provides:
  - a description of related *Previous work* covered in **NHM R**
  - a concise *Overview* of the work of the new topic
  - a *Development* section, which details the mathematical content and suggested teaching approaches for the topic

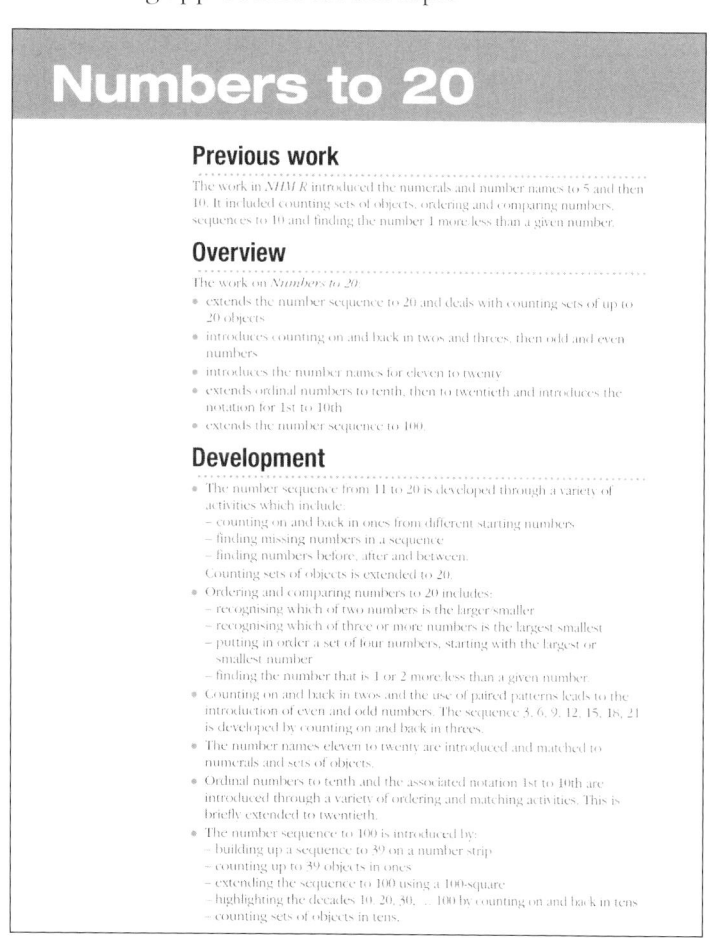

- a *Contents* table containing references to teacher and pupil materials required for each section within the topic
- a *Language* list of relevant mathematical vocabulary
- a *Resources* list, which outlines general items and appropriate materials from the *Teachers' Resource Pack*.

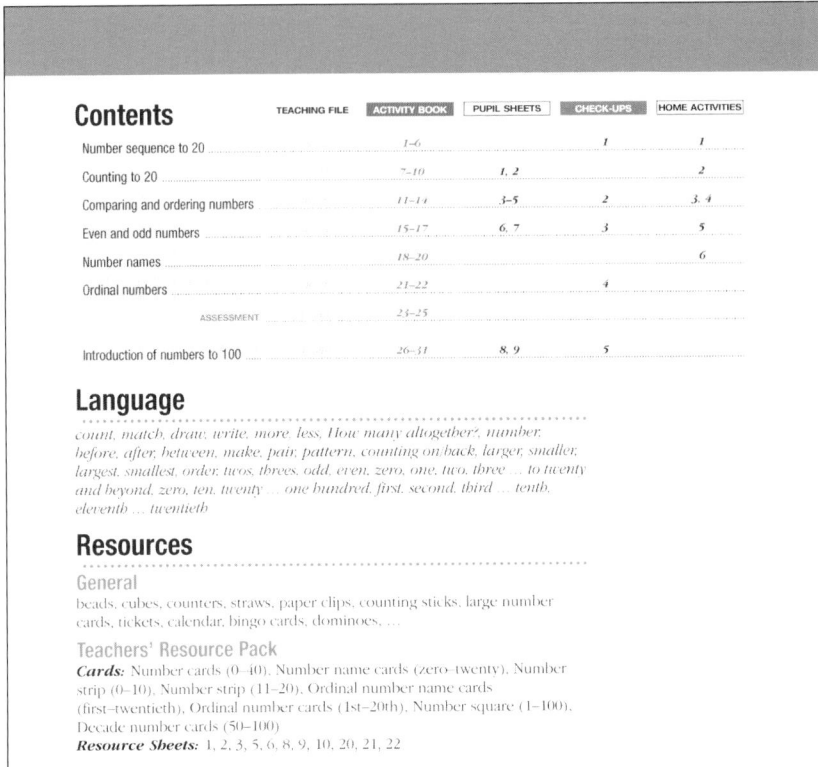

- The notes for each section within a topic follow the same pattern.

  A brief statement outlines the work covered by the section.

  A *Schematic* diagram details the lessons within the section. It shows how all the associated materials in **NHM 1** fit together and progress through the work of the section.

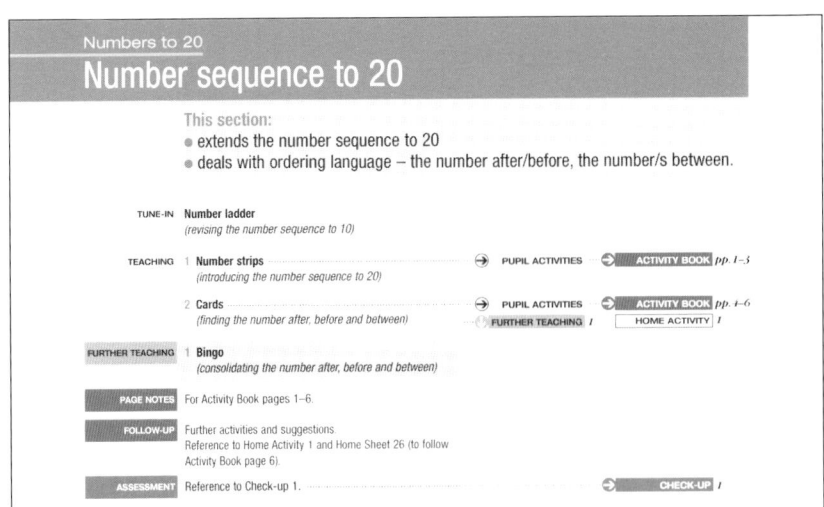

TUNE-IN

A *Tune-in* is then provided as a suggestion for starting the teaching. This is an interactive, mental, whole class activity which revises any relevant previous work and sets the scene for the first lesson of the section.

An activity from the bank of *Starters and other mental activities* can be used, if required, as a lead-in to subsequent lessons. Alternatively, an activity from the previous day's work can be adapted for this purpose.

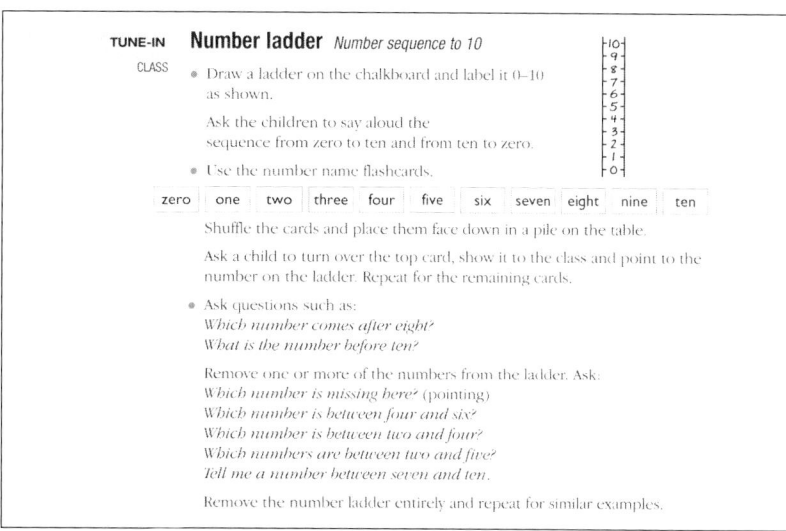

TEACHING

Teaching suggestions are given for class lessons to develop the sequence of work in the section.

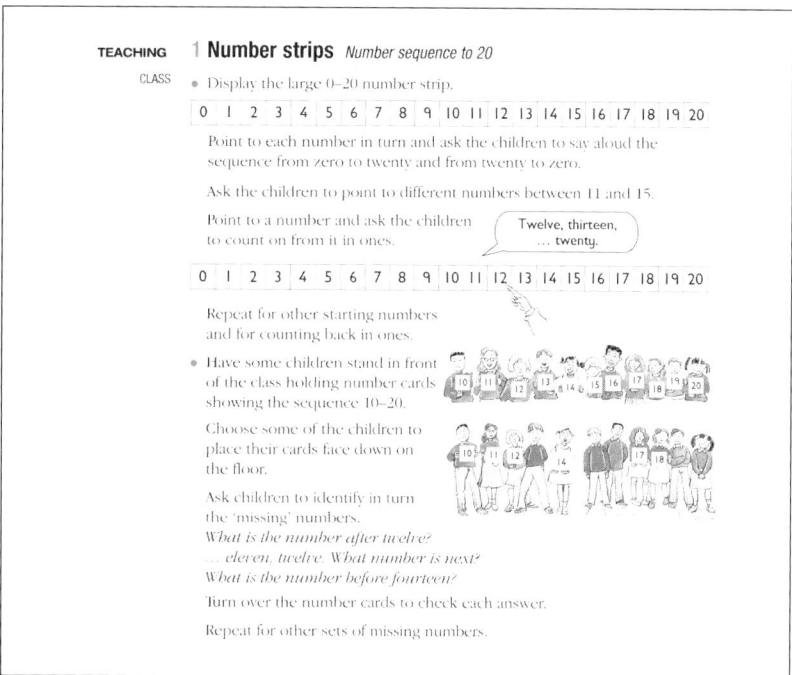

PUPIL ACTIVITIES

Pupil Activities, including practical activities, games and mental work, follow many of the lessons. These are designed to be used by groups, pairs or individuals, with some teacher support. When several activities are provided, a selection should be made to suit groups within the class.

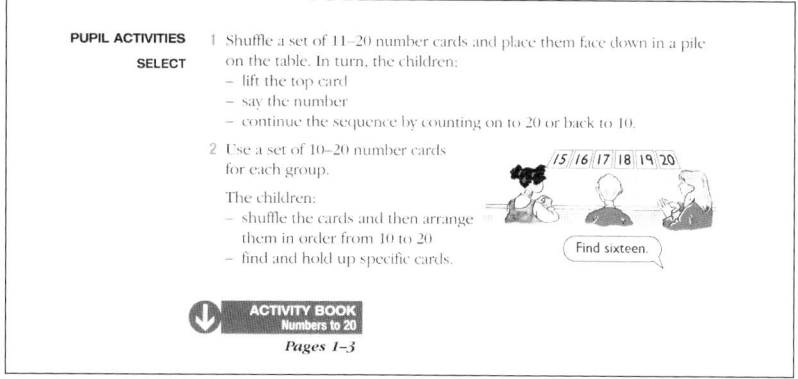

References to *Activity Book* pages point to appropriate written work for pupils.

ACTIVITY BOOK
Numbers to 20
Pages 1–3

References are given to *Further Teaching*, if any.

FURTHER TEACHING
2

Suggestions for *Further Teaching* lessons with the class or a group provide an alternative approach, consolidation or extension. The following occurs in the 'Comparing and ordering numbers' section of Numbers to 20.

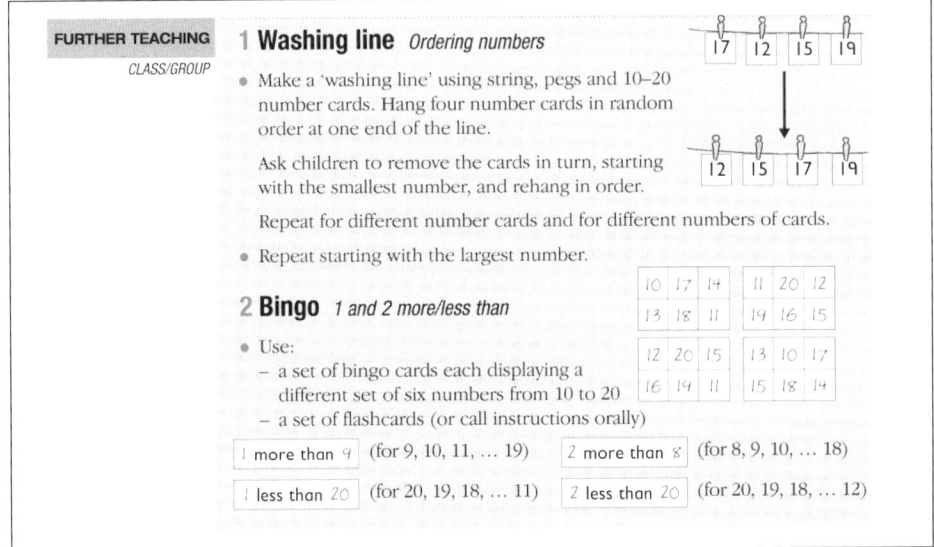

PAGE NOTES

Page Notes offer advice about using some of the relevant *Activity Book* pages. The notes highlight more challenging examples and possible difficulties with language and instructions.

FOLLOW-UP

Follow-up suggestions are given for drawing lessons to a close. These often involve whole class discussion, mental work, extension activities or further practice.

References are also given to:
– *Home Activities* related to the *Activity Book* pages
– *Pupil Sheets* which provide extra practice or extension.

ASSESSMENT

Where appropriate, the last heading in a section is *Assessment*.
This may include:
– a reference to a *Check-up* associated with the work of the section
– page notes for red-bordered, built-in assessment pages in an *Activity Book*.

The *Activity Book* assessment pages are designed to assess a number or money topic, covering the work of several sections. The notes point out some common errors that may occur and make some suggestions for dealing with them. For each question there are references to relevant *Activity Book* pages and the appropriate section of the *Teaching File,* should some re-teaching or additional practice be required.

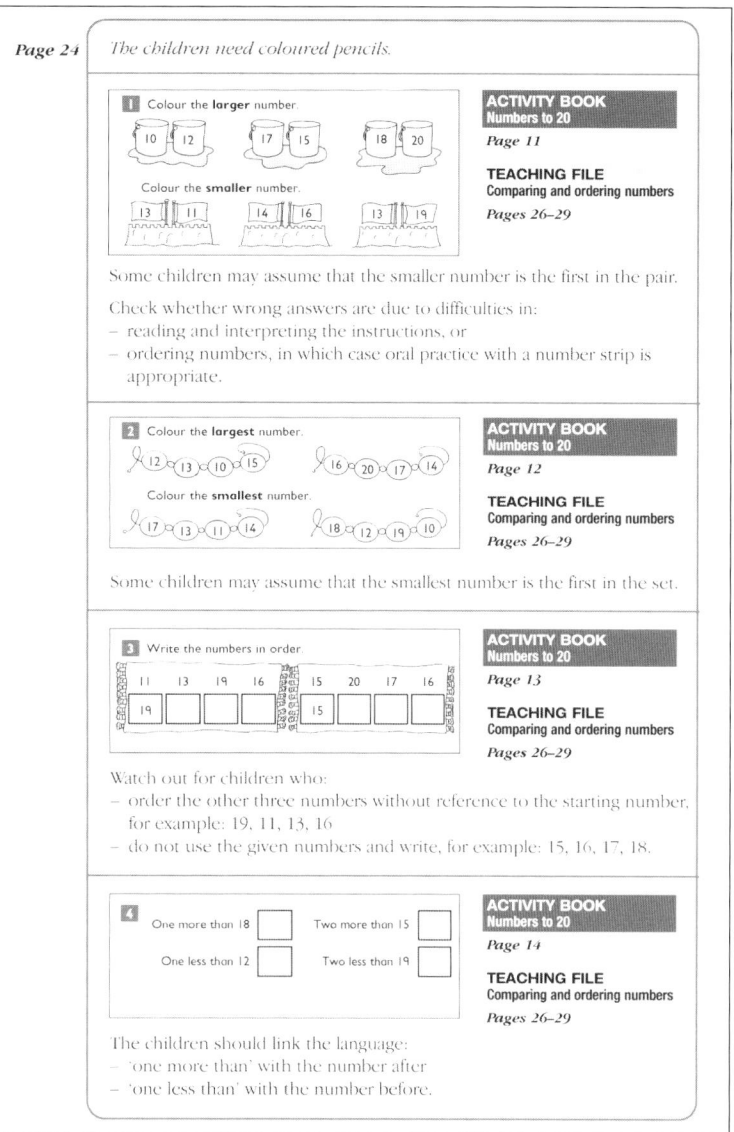

Page 24 The children need coloured pencils.

1 Colour the **larger** number.

Colour the **smaller** number.

ACTIVITY BOOK
Numbers to 20
Page 11

TEACHING FILE
Comparing and ordering numbers
Pages 26–29

Some children may assume that the smaller number is the first in the pair.

Check whether wrong answers are due to difficulties in:
– reading and interpreting the instructions, or
– ordering numbers, in which case oral practice with a number strip is appropriate.

2 Colour the **largest** number.

Colour the **smallest** number.

ACTIVITY BOOK
Numbers to 20
Page 12

TEACHING FILE
Comparing and ordering numbers
Pages 26–29

Some children may assume that the smallest number is the first in the set.

3 Write the numbers in order.

ACTIVITY BOOK
Numbers to 20
Page 13

TEACHING FILE
Comparing and ordering numbers
Pages 26–29

Watch out for children who:
– order the other three numbers without reference to the starting number, for example: 19, 11, 13, 16
– do not use the given numbers and write, for example: 15, 16, 17, 18.

4 One more than 18 ☐   Two more than 15 ☐
One less than 12 ☐   Two less than 19 ☐

ACTIVITY BOOK
Numbers to 20
Page 14

TEACHING FILE
Comparing and ordering numbers
Pages 26–29

The children should link the language:
– 'one more than' with the number after
– 'one less than' with the number before.

Pupil Sheets

- The **NHM 1** *Teaching File* includes 49 photocopiable *Pupil Sheets*. There are several types which have different purposes. For example:
  - to provide a means of recording during the course of a lesson
  - to give extra practice to children who have completed the *Activity Book* pages but need more examples
  - to follow up a lesson as consolidation, application or extension of what has been learned
  - to provide a template for teachers to produce their own sheets, which can be customised to cater for different ability levels.

Home Activities

- The **NHM 1** *Teaching File* contains 25 *Home Activities* and 2 *Home Sheets* of associated 'cards' for use with some of them. These are photocopiable.

  The activities aim to:
  - provide important extra practice for the child
  - give parents an opportunity to be actively involved with their child's learning and provide encouragement and help
  - inform those at home about the mathematics being taught in school.

- *Home Activities* are referenced from:
  - the foot of the *Activity Book* page which completes this work in school
  - the *Follow-up* section in the *Teaching File* for the related *Activity Book* page.

- There are two types of *Home Activity*:

  – simple oral, mental activities or games involving an adult and the child
    There are straight-forward instructions for the adult which give examples
    of the language to be used.
  – written practice examples for the child to complete and the adult to check.

Often both types appear on one sheet. However, it is not necessary to use
both parts at the same time.

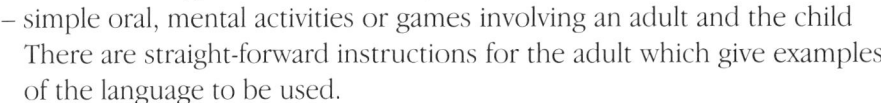

Activity Books

- There are five *Activity Books* for **NHM 1**:
    Numbers to 20
    Addition to 10
    Subtraction to 10
    Money
    Shape, Measure and Data Handling

- The *Activity Books* contain written work for the children for use after the
  Teaching of a lesson and related *Pupil Activities* have been completed. The
  pages have a fill-in format and provide practice, consolidation, application and
  extension work.

  The page on page 13 follows *Teaching* and *Pupil Activities* about 'Ordering
  and comparing numbers to 20'.

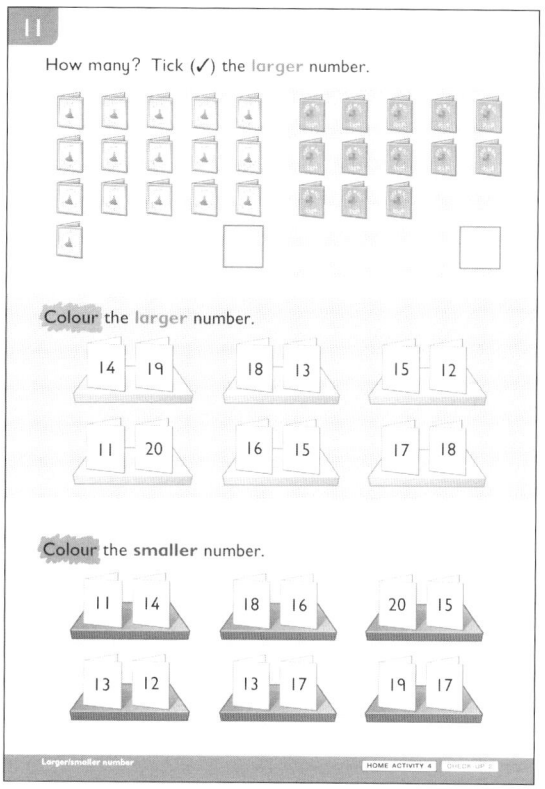

- There are references at the foot of some of the *Activity Book* pages to:
  – *Check-ups*, which assess one or two sections of work
  – *Home Activities*, which provide related work for a child and adult at home.

- In each *Activity Book* dealing with number or money, there are pages with red-borders. These contain wide-ranging assessments of several sections of work or a complete topic. The page below is one of three assessment pages in the Numbers to 20 *Activity Book*. As described on page 10, notes for such pages are given in the *Teaching File*.

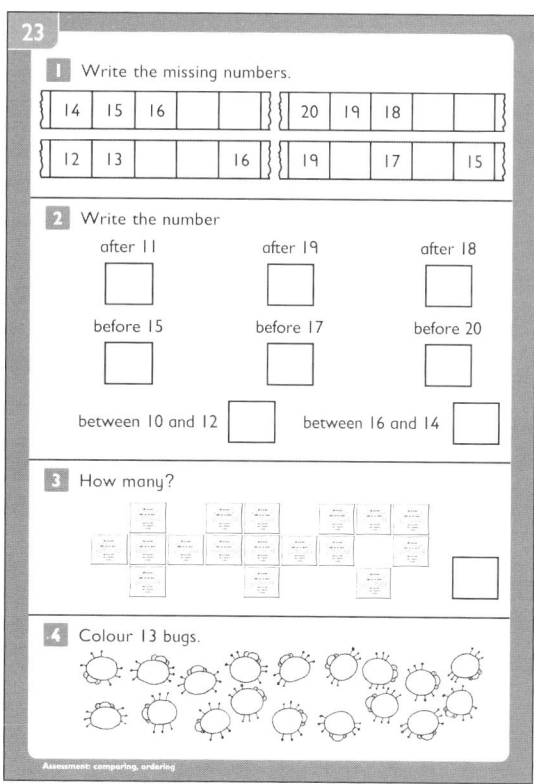

Check-ups

- The *Check-ups* are designed to assess children's understanding, knowledge and ability to apply skills and techniques. They are provided in booklet or photocopy master format. The **NHM 1** *Check-ups* contain:
  - 15 *Check-ups* covering the topics shown:
    - Numbers to 20 – 5
    - Addition to 10 – 5
    - Subtraction to 10 – 5
  - 2 *Round-ups*, containing questions on number, money, shape, measure and data handling.

- Each *Check-up* covers a smaller range of work within a single topic and is linked to the work on several *Activity Book* pages. One of the *Check-ups* for Numbers to 20 is shown below.

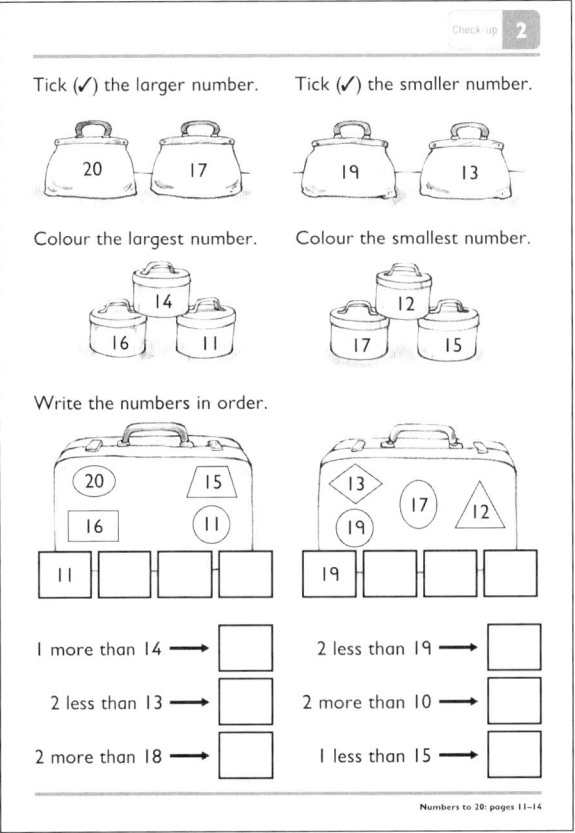

References to *Check-ups* are given in the *Teaching File* and at the foot of appropriate *Activity Book* pages.

- The *Round-ups* are end-of-year tests which cover a wide range of 'mixed' mathematics. They give an indication of overall level of attainment for the year.

Teachers' Resource Pack

- The pack contains two types of material:
  - ready-made cardboard aids such as flashcards, number cards, number lines, and so on, for use when teaching lessons or during pupil activities
  - a booklet of photocopiable *Resource Sheets* to produce further paper or card items for use with **NHM 1**.

Using New Heinemann Maths

Learning and teaching

The approach to learning and teaching in **NHM 1** is based on the following key ideas:
- daily mathematics lessons
- direct, interactive teaching
- systematic development of mental calculation.

Given this approach, the *Teaching File* is a crucial component of **NHM 1** as it provides guidance on:
- the development of each mathematical topic in a clear, systematic way
- teaching, pupil activities and follow-up work to promote understanding and develop and apply skills
- the effective use of resources to develop knowledge and understanding of key aspects of number work
- the use of mental and oral activities to develop and practise mental strategies and techniques.

Direct teaching is essential. It cannot be replaced by the use of *Pupil Sheets*, *Activity Books* and other course materials. The function of such materials is to:
- check the children's understanding of what has been taught
- provide a record of work completed
- set new challenges where the children can apply the mathematics they have learned.

The **NHM 1** pupil materials are **not** designed to teach new concepts to children working through them on their own, without prior teaching and discussion. The focus is very much on direct teaching and interaction.

Direct teaching and interaction

High quality direct teaching and interaction are at the heart of both the National Numeracy Strategy and **New Heinemann Maths**. This two-way process encourages both teachers and children to be actively engaged in the learning process.

Children are expected to:
- be actively involved in answering questions
- contribute to discussion during *Teaching* activities and *Follow-up* discussions
- be able to explain and demonstrate understanding of their learning to others.

The *Teaching File* makes suggestions which enable the teacher to provide an effective direct teaching approach through an appropriate balance of the following methods.

Demonstration – showing and illustrating mathematics using appropriate resources and visual materials.

Teaching File, page 18
Numbers to 20

TEACHING	1 **Number strips** *Number sequence to 20*
CLASS	• Display the large 0–20 number strip.
	0 1 2 3 4 5 6 7 8 9 10 11 12 13 14 15 16 17 18 19 20
	Point to each number in turn and ask the children to say aloud the sequence from zero to twenty and from twenty to zero.

Instruction – giving information clearly and precisely.

Teaching File, page 56
Addition to 10

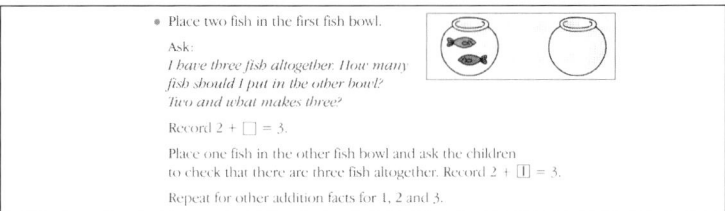

Direction – sharing teaching objectives with the children and making sure they know what they should be learning.

Teaching File, page 205
Weight

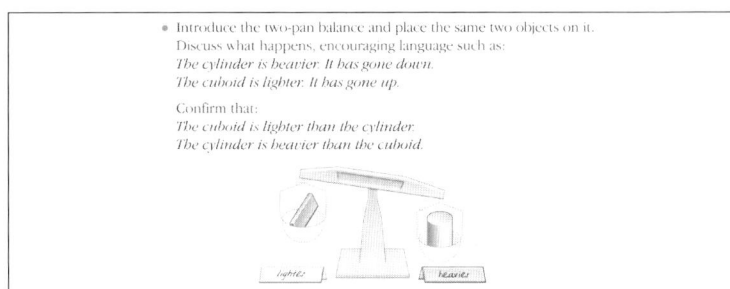

Explanation and illustration – giving accurate, well-paced explanations.

Teaching File, page 161
Subtraction to 10

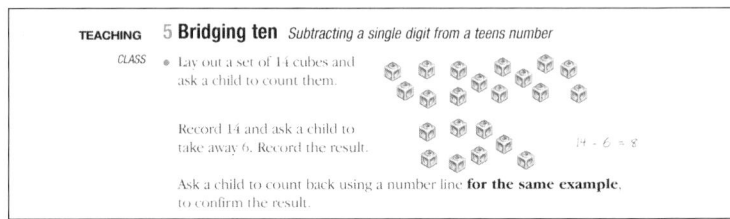

Questioning – using effective questioning techniques to:

- ensure that children are actively involved in their learning
- encourage the children to explain what they are doing
- help the children to consider other possible strategies and methods
- focus the children's attention on new aspects of their learning.

A wide range of open and closed questions are suggested within the *Teaching* activities in **NHM 1**.

Consolidating – maximising opportunities to reinforce and develop what has been taught through the use of:

- *Starters and other mental activities* to consolidate previous learning
- well-focused *Pupil Activities* and *Pupil Sheets*
- practice and applications in the *Activity Books*
- *Further Teaching* activities.

Discussion and evaluation of children's responses – identifying mistakes and misunderstandings by using:

- oral *Follow-up* activities from the *Teaching File*
- *Check-ups* in the *Check-ups* booklet
- red-bordered assessment pages in the *Activity Books*.

This process can help to identify appropriate further teaching.

Summarising – reviewing with the children what has been taught and what the children have learned using:

- *Follow-up* activities.

Differentiation

The National Numeracy Strategy states that the children should, as far as possible, work together through the year's programme described in the Framework. **New Heinemann Maths** has also been designed to be used in this way. However, there will be times when the teacher wishes to work with groups of children or individual children. The *Teaching* activities in the *Teaching File* have been written for whole class teaching, but can be adapted for use with groups or individuals.

The following features of **NHM 1** can help the teacher to plan differentiated programmes:

– the ability to select from the suggested *Teaching* activities, *Pupil Activities* and *Further Teaching* activities for each section in the *Teaching File* allows the teacher to plan appropriate programmes to match the children's needs

– *Pupil Sheets* provide further practice for those who need it. Some of them provide templates for teachers to customise for use with groups or individuals. The *Pupil Sheets* that follow some of the *Activity Book* pages should only be used by children who need additional consolidation.

The teacher should omit pages, parts of pages or questions in the *Activity Books* which are not appropriate for specific children. However, all children should have experience of using and applying the mathematics they are learning.

Planning

Starting points

Planning for effective learning involves thinking about:

– the National Numeracy Strategy.
   The chart on pages 28–33 summarises the curriculum coverage provided by **NHM 1**.

– the children's previous experience in mathematics.
   This can be found by consulting:
   ● the children's records of achievement
   ● the mathematical development chart on pages 40–43.

– the development of the children's knowledge, skills and understanding.

   Information relating to the work contained in **NHM 1** is found in:
   ● the pupil record grids on pages 46–48 of this guide.
   ● the summary at the beginning of each new topic in the *Teaching File*. It describes *Previous Work* and gives an *Overview* and a detailed *Development* of the topic. The *Contents* list gives the sections within the topic and all the **NHM 1** materials asssociated with them. The *Language* list gives a clear indication of the vocabulary used.

While there are many ways to plan a mathematics programme and schools will have their own planning formats, **NHM 1** provides examples of two types of year/term planner and one weekly planner. These are designed to provide a route through the materials. Year/term planners can be described in two ways: a 'framework planner' and a 'topic planner'.

Framework planner

The framework planner identifies each unit of work within the National Numeracy Strategy in order, and the objectives that are being addressed. This is then matched to the appropriate sections of **NHM 1**.

Detailed autumn, spring and summer planners are included on pages 28–33 of this guide.

Appendix A: Framework planner

Year 1: Autumn

Unit	Framework Topic	Objectives: children will be taught to …	NHM Topic	NHM Section	Teaching File page	Date/Comments
1	Counting, properties of number and number sequences	● Know the number names and recite them in order to at least 20, from and back to zero	Numbers to 20	● **Number sequence to 20:** – extends the number sequence to 20. ● **Number names:** – introduces names eleven to twenty.	18–19 35–37	
2–4	Place value and ordering	● **Read and write numerals from 0 to at least 20** ● **Understand and use the vocabulary of comparing and ordering numbers** Compare two familiar numbers and give a number which lies between them	Numbers to 20	● **Number sequence to 20:** – extends the number sequence to 20 – deals with ordering language – the number after/before, the number(s) between.	19–22	
	Understanding + and – Mental calculation strategies (+ and –)	● **Understand the operation of addition and use the related vocabulary** ● Begin to use the + and = signs to record mental calculations in a number sentence and to recognise the use of symbols such as □ or △ to stand for an unknown number ● Know by heart: addition facts for all pairs of numbers with a total up to at least 5 addition doubles of all numbers to at least 5 (e.g. 4 + 4) ● Identify near doubles, using doubles already known (e.g. 6 + 5) ● Begin to recognise that more than two numbers can be added together	Addition to 10	● **Addition to 5: consolidation:** – consolidates addition facts to 5 and includes the addition of three numbers – introduces examples of the type 2 + □ = 5 and □ + 1 = 5. ● **Doubles and near doubles:** – systematically introduces 'doubles' and 'near doubles' facts for addition to 10 – deals with the development of quick random recall of these facts.	54–58 59–63	
5–6	Money and 'real life' problems Making decisions	● **Use mental strategies to solve simple problems** set in 'real life' using addition ● Recognise coins of different values Find totals and change from up to 20p	Money	● **Addition to 10p/£10:** – introduces addition to 10p/£10 using coins, then mentally.	164–166	
	Measures	● Understand and use the vocabulary related to length, including problems ● **Compare two lengths by direct comparison;** extend to more than two ● **Suggest suitable non-standard units and measuring equipment to estimate, then measure a length**	Length	● **Length:** – introduces direct comparison of lengths using language such as longer, shorter, … longest, shortest, … – introduces the use of arbitrary and non-standard units to measure and compare lengths – deals with estimation, and selection of suitable measuring units.	195–201	
	Shape and Space Reasoning about shapes	● **Use everyday language to describe features of familiar 3-D shapes,** including the cube, sphere, cylinder, cone, referring to properties such as the shape of flat faces, or the number of faces or corners… ● Make and describe models, patterns and pictures using construction kits, everyday materials, Plasticine… Begin to relate solid shapes to pictures of them ● Use everyday language to describe position, direction and movement ● Investigate a general statement about familiar shapes by finding examples that satisfy it ● Explain methods and reasoning orally	3D Shape	● **3D Shape:** – deals with recognising and naming 3D shapes using: – 'everyday' names (cube, box, ball, cone, tube) – mathematical names (cube, cuboid, sphere, cone, cylinder) – introduces language associated with 3D shapes (rolls, slides, flat, curved, face, edge, straight, corner) – deals with language associated with position (near, beside, below, under, above).	180–184	
7	Assess and review		Assess and review			

Topic planner

This planner takes an alternative approach by illustrating a progression in the teaching of each maths topic and matching the numeracy objectives to it. Each term has been subdivided into the same number of units as the framework planner.

Detailed autumn, spring and summer planners are included on pages 34–39 of this guide.

Appendix B: Topic planner

Year 1: Autumn

Unit	NHM Topic	NHM Section	Teaching File page	Framework Topic	Objectives: children will be taught to …	Date/Comments
1–4	Numbers to 20	● **Number sequence to 20:** – extends the number sequence to 20 – deals with ordering language – the number after/before, the number(s) between – introduces counting and drawing up to 20 objects – introduces counting a number of objects within a set.	18–19 23–25	Counting, properties of number and number sequences	● Know the number names and recite them in order to at least 20, from and back to zero ● **Count reliably at least 20 objects** ● **Read and write numerals from 0 to at least 20** ● Recognise and predict from simple patterns and relationships.	
		● **Comparing and ordering numbers:** – deals with recognising the larger/smaller number in a pair – deals with recognising the largest/smallest number in a set of three – includes ordering up to five non-consecutive numbers, starting with the largest/smallest – includes finding a number 1 and 2 more/less than a given number.	26–29	Place value and ordering	● **Understand and use the vocabulary of comparing and ordering numbers** Compare two familiar numbers, say which is more or less, and give a number which lies between them ● **Order numbers to at least 20;** and position them on a number track.	
		● **Even and odd numbers:** – deals with counting on and back in steps of 2 – introduces even and odd numbers – introduces counting on and back in steps of 3.	30–34	Counting, properties of number and number sequences	● Describe and extend number sequences: count on in twos from zero, then one, and begin to recognise odd or even numbers to about 20 begin to count on in steps of 3 from zero.	
		● **Number names:** – introduces number names eleven to twenty. ● **Ordinal numbers:** – introduces fourth, fifth, sixth, … tenth – introduces the notation 1st, 2nd, 3rd, … 10th.	35–37 38–40	Place value and ordering	● Know the number names and recite them in order to at least 20 ● **Understand and use the vocabulary of comparing and ordering numbers,** including ordinal numbers to at least 20.	
5	Length	● **Length:** – introduces direct comparison of lengths using language such as longer, shorter, … longest, shortest, … – introduces the use of arbitrary and non-standard units to measure and compare lengths – deals with estimation, and selection of suitable measuring units.	195–201	Measures, including problems	● Understand and use the vocabulary related to length ● **Compare two lengths by direct comparison;** extend to more than two ● **Suggest suitable non-standard units and measuring equipment to estimate, then measure a length.**	
6	3D Shape	● **3D Shape:** – deals with recognising and naming 3D shapes using: – 'everyday' names (cube, box, ball, cone, tube) – mathematical names (cube, cuboid, sphere, cone, cylinder) – introduces language associated with 3D shapes (rolls, slides, flat, curved, face, edge, straight, corner) – deals with language associated with position (near, beside, below, under, above).	180–184	Shape and Space Reasoning about shapes	● **Use everyday language to describe features of familiar 3-D shapes,** including the cube, sphere, cylinder, cone, referring to properties such as the shape of flat faces, or the number of faces or corners… ● Make and describe models, patterns and pictures using contruction kits, everyday materials, Plasticine… Begin to relate solid shapes to pictures of them ● Investigate a general statement about familiar shapes by finding examples that satisfy it ● Use everyday language to describe position, direction and movement.	
7	Assess and review			Assess and review		

Weekly planner

It is often necessary to plan in more detail on a weekly or daily basis. Plans of this type provide an indication of what the teacher hopes to cover during the course of the week. However, given that the mathematics must necessarily build on the needs of the children, an element of flexibility should be built in. This allows for modification to the plan as it is implemented.

The *Schematic* diagrams at the beginning of each section in the *Teaching File* provide a helpful starting point for this process.

Teaching File, page 54
Addition to 10

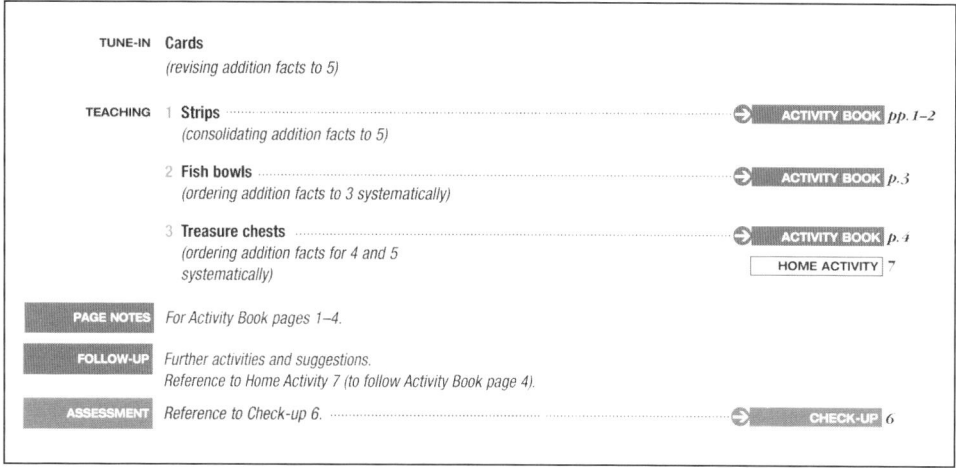

Teaching File, page 59
Addition to 10

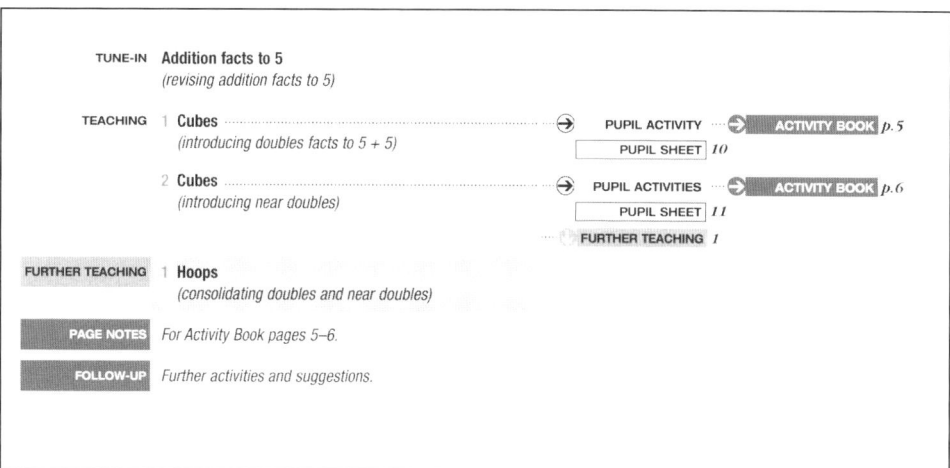

The weekly planner on page 20 shows how two sections of Addition to 10 might be developed over the course of a week.

Weekly Planner: Understanding addition and subtraction

SECTION	Revising addition facts to 5			Doubles and near doubles	
	Monday	**Tuesday**	**Wednesday**	**Thursday**	**Friday**
TUNE-IN or **STARTER**	**Tune-in Cards** Revising addition facts to 5	Activity from *Starters and other mental activities*	Activity from *Starters and other mental activities*	**Tune-in Addition facts for 5**	Activity from *Starters and other mental activities*
TEACHING	**1 Strips** *T.F. 54–55* • Building addition facts to 5 • Revising language 'and', 'add' • Examples □ + □ = 5	**2 Fish bowls** *T.F. 55* • Systematising facts for 1, 2, 3 • Introducing examples of the type 2 + □ = 3	**3 Treasure chests** *T.F. 56–57* • Systematising addition facts for 4, 5 • Introducing examples of the type □ + 1 = 4	**1 Cubes** *T.F. 59–60* • Introducing doubles facts to 5 + 5	**1 Cubes** *T.F. 60–62* • Introducing near doubles using towers of cubes
PUPIL ACTIVITIES	**Activity Book** *Pages 1–2*	**Activity Book** *Page 3*	**Activity Book** *Page 4* **Check-up 6**	**Pupil activity:** 1 Doubles strips **Pupil Sheet 10** **Activity Book** *Page 5*	**Pupil activities:** **Pupil Sheet 11** *and/or* Matching game **Activity Book** *Page 6*
FOLLOW-UP	For **Activity Book page 2** Showing different totals to 5	For **Activity Book page 3** Saying whether additions are ✔ or ✘	Repeat activity from *Starters and other mental activities*	For **Activity Book page 5** Tell me the double of this number	**Further Teaching 1 Hoops** *or* For **Activity Book page 6** **Oral practice of double facts**
REVIEW	***This would include:*** – *key areas of concern to build into the next day's teaching* – *any organisation issues to be addressed* – *any child needing particular help.*				

Organising and using the materials

- In the summary at the beginning of each new topic in the *Teaching File* there is a list of *Resources* required for the topic.

> ## Resources
>
> ### General
> interlocking cubes, counters, beads, tubs, trays, boxes, toy cars, envelopes, 2 large dice, cards showing a large 'leaf', 2 'socks', 4 'fish' and 5 'bottles', large dominoes for double 3, 4 and 5, subtraction cards such as 8–3, picture cards with 6–10 objects on them, a large partitioned set, paired dot patterns to 6, …
>
> ### Teachers' Resource Pack
> **Cards:** Number cards (0–40), Number strip (0–10), Number line (0–10), Number line (11–20), Ten-frame cards (blank), Ten-frame cards (0–10)
> **Resource Sheets:** 3, 4, 5, 6, 8, 9, 10, 15, 16, 17, 18, 20

These are listed under two headings – *General* and *Teachers' Resource Pack*.

The *General* resources list the types of practical materials that are normally to be found in early years' classrooms. These resources should be easily accessible to the children.

The *Teachers' Resource Pack* list includes:
– the specific resouces such as number lines, ten-frames and so on, that are provided, ready to use, with **NHM 1**. These are card materials, designed for use by the teacher.
– photocopiable *Resource Sheets* that teachers may wish to use in this section of teaching. These materials are designed to be used by the children.

Other resources such as the necessary *Pupil Sheets*, *Check-ups* and *Home Activities* are listed in the *Contents* table for the topic and the schematic diagrams for each section.

Contents

	TEACHING FILE	ACTIVITY BOOK	PUPIL SHEETS	CHECK-UPS	HOME ACTIVITIES
Concept of subtraction		1–2	18		
Subtraction involving 1, 2 and 0		3–4			11
Facts to 5		5–7	19, 20		12
Subtraction language		8–11		11	13, 14
ASSESSMENT		12			
Subtraction within 10		13–17	21		15
Facts for 6 and 7		18–20			16, 17
Facts for 8 and 9		21–24		12	18, 19
Facts to 10		25–27	22, 23	13	20, 21
Subtraction: comparison		28–30	24, 25		22
Linking + and – facts for 6 to 10		31–32	26, 27		23
Subtraction facts to 10		33–34		14	
ASSESSMENT		35–36			
Subtraction beyond 10		37–39	28, 29	15	

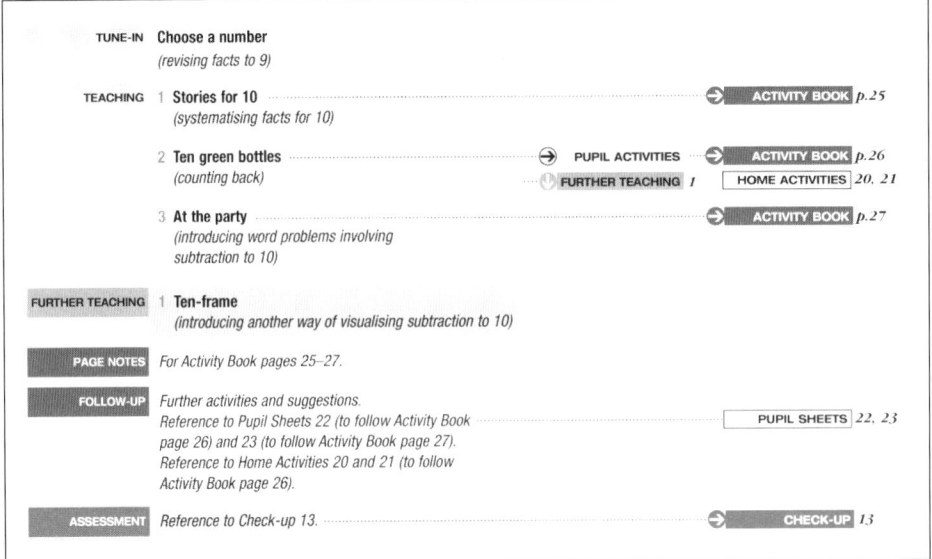

- The materials in **New Heinemann Maths** allow the teacher to structure each mathematics lesson in the three clear parts as described in the National Numeracy Strategy. These are:

  – **oral work and mental calculation** using the appropriate *Tune-in*, or an activity from the *Starters and other mental activities* section of the *Teaching File*

  – **the main teaching activity** using *Teaching* and *Pupil Activities*, *Pupil Sheets* and appropriate pages of the *Activity Book,* described and illustrated in the *Teaching File*

  – **a plenary** using further activities and suggestions, for example, from the *Follow-up* to *Activity Book* pages as suggested in the *Teaching File*. The *Follow-up* section also indicates appropriate *Home Activities*.

  The teaching suggestions given in the *Teaching File* do not indicate approximate timings for each part of the lesson. Professional judgement must be used to determine the most appropriate pacing, organisation and specific activities to best meet the needs of the children and the topic. Some flexibility is needed to take account of the children's learning.

- The *Tune-in*, *Teaching* and *Pupil Activities* should be completed before the children attempt related *Activity Book* pages.

  When the children are ready to attempt the *Activity Book* page it may be necessary for the teacher to discuss some of the following:
  – what the children have to do, focusing on any concerns with language or the interpretation of instructions
  – where to find any materials they may need
  – how they should set out work or record answers
  – which questions they should complete or omit.

  Teachers, on occasion, may want to ask the children to:
  – do the examples on an *Activity Book* page orally without keeping a written record
  – interpret an example in their own words
  – work in pairs or small groups with only one child recording the answers.

  Sometimes it may be appropriate to tackle a page as a class discussion with each child writing answers as they go along.

- The plenary is an important part of the lesson. During this time the teacher may wish to:
  - ask children to show and explain their work to other children
  - draw together what has been learned and, on occasion, extend the work through oral discussion
  - provide tasks for the children to complete at home to consolidate their work in class using, for example, a *Home Activity*
  - make connections to other areas of the curriculum that the children will encounter during the day.

5 Assessment

Day-by-day

Much of the assessment of children's learning of mathematics in the primary classroom is of an informal nature and happens on a daily basis. This can be done during many of the activities that children are involved in such as:
- the *Tune-in* or *Starters and other mental activities*
- the main *Teaching* activity
- the *Pupil Activities*, including games, practical activities, *Pupil Sheets* and *Activity Books*
- the *Follow-up* discussion highlighting the main teaching ideas.

These provide evidence which the teacher can use to determine the level of a child's understanding of a particular mathematical idea. The evidence is gathered in a number of different ways over a period of time by:
- listening to and talking with the children (posing questions and noting responses)
- observing the children (noting individual strengths and needs)
- correcting the children's written work
- using the children's self-assessment.

However, more focused methods of assessment are also necessary. **NHM 1** provides:
- *Check-ups* to assess the children's understanding of a section of work they have recently completed
- red-bordered assessment pages in the *Activity Books* to assess a mathematical topic
- *Round-ups* to assess the children's understanding of the range of the mathematics they have been involved in during the course of the year.

Focused assessment

Check-ups

When the teacher wishes to use a more objective, specific task to check on the children's understanding of a particular section of teaching in mathematics, for example 'Comparing and ordering numbers to 20', one of the *Check-ups*, can be used. These are provided in booklet and photocopiable format.

A *Check-up* will normally be used after a section of work has been completed. The *Schematics* and *Contents* tables in the summary pages indicate which *Check-up* relates to a particular section of work and when it should be used. The teaching notes give details of the mathematics covered and the relevant *Activity Book* pages for each *Check-up*.

 **ASSESSMENT** CHECK-UP 2 — Check-up 2 can be used to assess the work on *Comparing and ordering numbers* including larger/smaller and largest/smallest numbers, ordering and 1 and 2 more/less. The check-up is related to the work completed in the Numbers to 20 Activity Book, pages 11–14.

These notes follow the *Page Notes* and suggestions for *Follow-up* activities. These *Check-ups* provide a valuable record of achievement/attainment that can:

– highlight where further teaching and consolidation may be necessary
– be discussed with the child
– be used as a focus of discussion with parents
– be transferred along with other evidence to another teacher or school.

Red-bordered Activity Book assessment pages

Each of the Number and Money *Activity Books* (Numbers to 20, Addition to 10, Subtraction to 10, Money) contains assessment pages which assess the work related to a specific number topic, such as Numbers to 20.

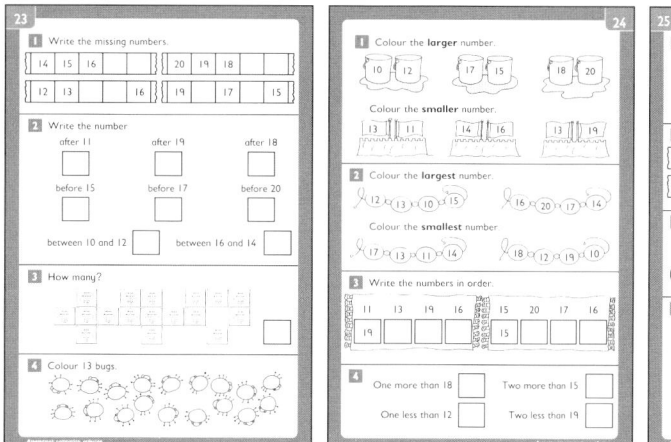

These pages are easily identified by the solid red border around the whole page. This type of assessment is normally used when a whole topic has been completed.

The *Schematic* diagram at the start of each section indicates where these assessments occur and when they should be used.

The teaching notes give details of:

– the mathematics covered and the relevant *Activity Book* pages

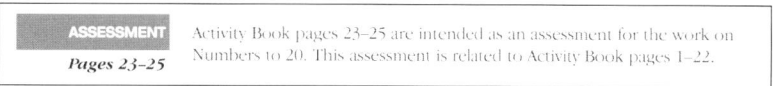

| ASSESSMENT | Activity Book pages 23–25 are intended as an assessment for the work on |
| Pages 23–25 | Numbers to 20. This assessment is related to Activity Book pages 1–22. |

– specific equipment or materials

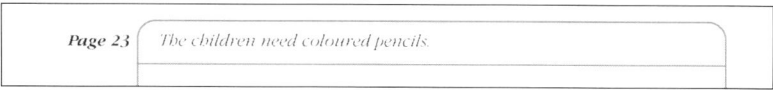

| Page 23 | The children need coloured pencils. |

– what each question is assessing and any common errors children may make
– brief suggestions about how to deal with some repeated errors
– references to the appropriate section of the *Teaching File* to return to if further teaching or consolidation is required.

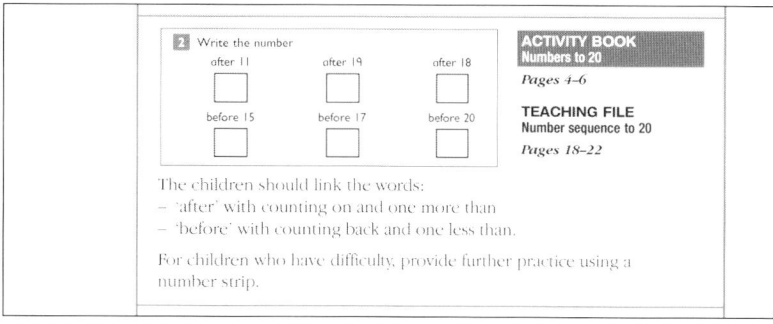

Round-up assessments

The two end-of-year *Round-up* assessments check on the full range of the mathematics covered.

These *Round-ups* are provided in the *Check-ups* booklet.

Round-up 1 includes questions related to Numbers to 20, Addition to 10, Subtraction to 10, Money, 2D Shape, Length, Time and Data Handling.

Round-up 2 includes questions related to Numbers to 20, Addition to 10, Subtraction to 10, Money, 2D Shape, Time and Weight.

Completion of both *Round-ups* provides evidence of how well the children have achieved the National Numeracy Strategy *Framework for teaching mathematics* key objectives for Year 1.

Using the assessment materials

The *Check-ups*, *Activity Book* assessment pages and *Round-ups* provide useful information on:
- an individual child's progress, noting areas of success and highlighting specific areas of difficulty
- how the class or groups of children are progressing, indicating success or common difficulties that have emerged which require attention.

For example, discussion with the children about their work on a particular *Check-up* may help to establish why specific questions proved difficult. From this discussion important teaching points may be identified.

One copy of the *Check-ups* could be used to record specific comments about common difficulties. For example, using a highlighter pen to indicate questions where a significant number of children had experienced difficulty, or by circling questions where no errors occurred.

Recording progress

Assessment record grid

An assessment record grid is provided on page 44 of this guide to help record class, group or individual coverage of the *Check-ups*, *Activity Book* assessment pages and *Round-ups* completed. Ways of recording coverage might include a tick (✓) or a qualitative indicator of how well a specific assessment was completed. This could be done by shading part or all of an individual box. For example:

☐ no errors made

◪ few errors made

◼ a significant number of errors made.

Key objectives class assessment grid

Page 45 provides a simple checklist of the key objectives for Year 1. Space is provided to note work which has been attempted and the quality of the performances of the individuals within the class.

This class record grid enables the teacher to monitor the progress of the whole class.

Record of work grids

Record of work grids are provided on pages 46–48 of this *Organising and Planning Guide*. These grids can be used to show:
– when work has been completed
– how well the work has been completed, for example by using a code.

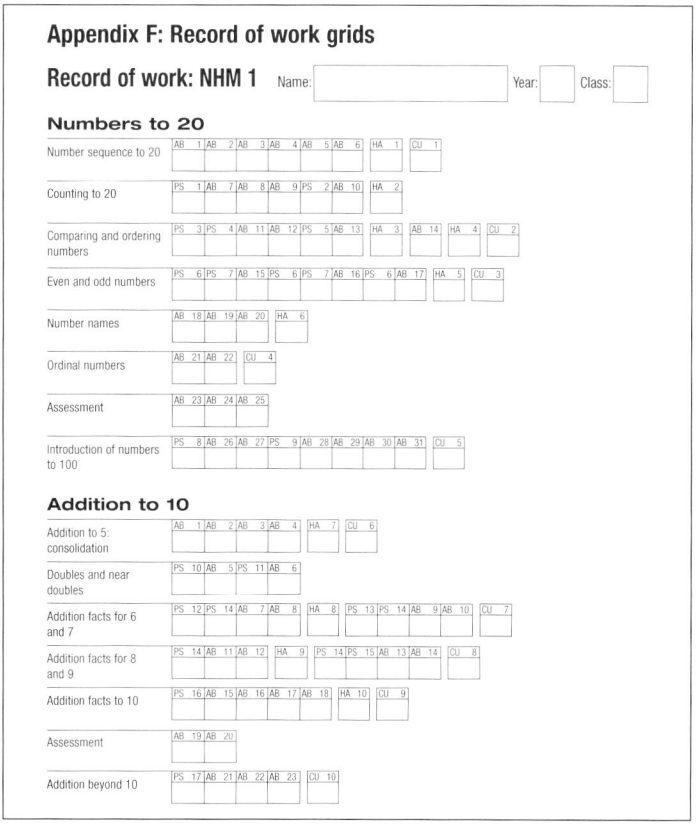

7 Appendices

Appendix A: Framework planner

Unit	Framework Topic	Objectives: children will be taught to ...
1	Counting, properties of number and number sequences	• Know the number names and recite them in order to at least 20, from and back to zero
2–4	Place value and ordering	• **Read and write numerals from 0 to at least 20** • **Understand and use the vocabulary of comparing and ordering numbers** Compare two familiar numbers and give a number which lies between them
	Understanding + and – Mental calculation strategies (+ and –)	• **Understand the operation of addition and use the related vocabulary** • Begin to use the + and = signs to record mental calculations in a number sentence and to recognise the use of symbols such as □ or △ to stand for an unknown number • Know by heart: addition facts for all pairs of numbers with a total up to at least 5 addition doubles of all numbers to at least 5 (e.g. 4 + 4) • Identify near doubles, using doubles already known (e.g. 6 + 5) • Begin to recognise that more than two numbers can be added together
	Money and 'real life' problems Making decisions	• **Use mental strategies to solve simple problems** set in 'real life' **using addition** • Recognise coins of different values Find totals and change from up to 20p
5–6	Measures	• Understand and use the vocabulary related to length, including problems • **Compare two lengths by direct comparison;** extend to more than two • **Suggest suitable non-standard units and measuring equipment to estimate, then measure a length**
	Shape and Space Reasoning about shapes	• **Use everyday language to describe features of familiar 3-D shapes**, including the cube, sphere, cylinder, cone, referring to properties such as the shape of flat faces, or the number of faces or corners… • Make and describe models, patterns and pictures using construction kits, everyday materials, Plasticine… Begin to relate solid shapes to pictures of them • Use everyday language to describe position, direction and movement • Investigate a general statement about familiar shapes by finding examples that satisfy it • Explain methods and reasoning orally
7	Assess and review	

Unit	Framework Topic	Objectives: children will be taught to ...
8	Counting, properties of number and number sequences Reasoning about numbers	• **Count reliably at least 20 objects** • Recognise and predict from simple patterns and relationships
9–11	Place value, ordering, estimating	• **Understand and use vocabulary of comparing and ordering numbers** • **Order numbers to at least 20** and position them on a number track
	Understanding + and – Mental calculation strategies (+ and –)	• **Understand the operation of addition and use the related vocabulary** Begin to recognise that addition can be done in any order Begin to use the + and = signs to record mental calculation in a number sentence, and to recognise the use of symbols such as □ or △ to stand for an unknown number • **Know by heart all pairs of numbers with a total of 10** (e.g. 3 + 7) • Use patterns of similar calculations (e.g. 10 – 0 = 10, 10 – 1 = 9, 10 – 2 = 8 …) • Use known number facts to add a pair of numbers mentally within the range 0 to at least 10
	Money and 'real life' problems Making decisions	• Recognise coins of different values Find totals and change from up to 20p Work out how to pay an exact sum using smaller coins • Explain methods and reasoning orally
12–13	Measures and time, including problems	• Understand and use the vocabulary related to time Know the days of the week
	Handling data	• Solve a given problem by sorting, classifying and organising information in simple ways, such as: using objects or pictures Discuss and explain results
14	Assess and review	

NHM Topic	NHM Section	Teaching File page	Date/Comments
Numbers to 20	● **Number sequence to 20:** – extends the number sequence to 20. ● **Number names:** – introduces names eleven to twenty.	18–19 35–37	
Numbers to 20	● **Number sequence to 20:** – extends the number sequence to 20 – deals with ordering language – the number after/before, the number(s) between.	19–22	
Addition to 10	● **Addition to 5: consolidation:** – consolidates addition facts to 5 and includes the addition of three numbers – introduces examples of the type 2 + □ = 5 and □ + 1 = 5. ● **Doubles and near doubles:** – systematically introduces 'doubles' and 'near doubles' facts for addition to 10 – deals with the development of quick random recall of these facts.	54–58 59–63	
Money	● **Addition to 10p/£10:** – introduces addition to 10p/£10 using coins, then mentally.	164–166	
Length	● **Length:** – introduces direct comparison of lengths using language such as longer, shorter, … longest, shortest, … – introduces the use of arbitrary and non-standard units to measure and compare lengths – deals with estimation, and selection of suitable measuring units.	195–201	

3D Shape	● **3D Shape:**
	– deals with recognising and naming 3D shapes using:
	  – 'everyday' names (cube, box, ball, cone, tube)
	  – mathematical names (cube, cuboid, sphere, cone, cylinder)
	– introduces language associated with 3D shapes (rolls, slides, flat, curved, face, edge, straight, corner)
	– deals with language associated with position (near, beside, below, under, above).
		180–184	

Assess and review			
Numbers to 20	● **Counting to 20:** – introduces counting and drawing up to 20 objects – introduces counting a number of objects within a set.	23–25	
Numbers to 20	● **Comparing and ordering numbers:** – deals with recognising the larger/smaller number in a pair – deals with recognising the largest/smallest number in a set of three.	26–27	
Addition to 10	● **Addition facts for 6 and 7:** – introduces systematically the addition facts for 6 and 7 – develops quick, random recall of these facts and all previously learned. ● **Addition facts for 8 and 9:** – introduces systematically the addition facts for 8 and 9 – develops quick, random recall of these facts and other facts previously learned. ● **Addition facts to 10:** – introduces systematically the addition facts for 10 – develops quick, random recall of all facts to 10.	64–79	
Money	● **Using 1p, 2p and 5p coins:** – gives practice in using 1p, 2p and 5p coins – deals with finding totals of combinations of 1p, 2p and 5p coins – introduces selecting coins to pay the exact amount for an item.	171–175	
Time	● **Days of the week:** – introduces the days of the week.	214–217	
Data Handling	● **Sorting, matching, relationships:** – encourages children to select their own criteria for sorting	230–232	
Assess and review			

Framework planner

Unit	Framework Topic	Objectives: children will be taught to ...
1	**Counting, properties of number and number sequences**	● Count on in twos from zero, then one, and begin to recognise odd or even numbers to about 20; begin to count on in steps of 3 from zero.
2–4	**Place value and ordering**	● **Understand and use the vocabulary of comparing and ordering numbers** Compare two familiar numbers, say which is more or less, and give a number which lies between them
	Understanding + and – **Mental calculation strategies (+ and –)**	● **Understand the operation of subtraction (as 'take away', 'difference', and 'how many more') and use the related vocabulary** ● Begin to use the – and = signs to record mental calculation in a number sentence, and to recognise the use of symbols such as □ or △ to stand for an unknown number ● **Know by heart** subtraction facts for all pairs of numbers with a total up to at least 5
	Money and 'real life' problems **Making decisions**	● **Use mental strategies to solve simple problems** set in 'real life' **using subtraction, explaining methods and reasoning orally.**
5–6	**Measures including problems**	● Understand and use the vocabulary related to mass **Compare two masses by direct comparison;** extend to more than two ● **Suggest suitable non-standard units and measuring equipment to estimate, then measure a mass.**
	Shape and Space **Reasoning about shapes**	● **Use everyday language to describe features of familiar 2-D shapes**, including the circle, triangle, square, rectangle ..., referring to properties such as the number of corners or the number and types of sides ● Make and describe models, patterns and pictures using construction kits, everyday materials and Plasticine... ● Investigate a general statement about familiar shapes by finding examples that satisfy it.
7	**Assess and review**	
8	**Counting, properties of number and number sequences**	● Know the number names and recite them in order to at least 20
9–10	**Place value and ordering**	● **Understand and use the vocabulary of comparing and ordering numbers**, including ordinal numbers to at least 20
	Understanding + and – **Mental calculation strategies (+ and –)**	● **Understand the operation of subtraction and use the related vocabulary** Begin to use the – and = signs to record mental calculations in a number sentence, and to recognise the use of symbols such as □ or △ to stand for an unknown number ● Begin to know subtraction facts for all pairs of numbers with a total up to at least 10 ● Use patterns of similar calculations (e.g. $10 - 0 = 10$, $10 - 1 = 9$, $10 - 2 = 8$ ...) ● Use known number facts to subtract a pair of numbers mentally within the range 0 to at least 10
11–12	**Measures and time, including problems**	● Understand and use the vocabulary related to time Read the time to the hour or half hour on analogue clocks
	Handling data	● Solve a given problem by sorting, classifying and organising information in simple ways, such as: using objects or pictures Discuss and explain results
13	**Assess and review**	

NHM Topic	NHM Section	Teaching File page	Date/Comments
Numbers to 20	● **Even and odd numbers:** – deals with counting on and back in steps of 2 – introduces even and odd numbers – introduces counting on and back in steps of 3.	30–34	
Numbers to 20	● **Comparing and ordering numbers:** – ordering up to five non-consecutive numbers, starting with the largest/smallest – finding a number 1 and 2 more/less than a given number.	27–29	
Subtraction to 10	● **Concept of subtraction:** – deals with the concept of subtraction – introduces the language 'take away' and the '−' symbol.	92–95	
	● **Subtraction involving 1, 2 and 0:** – deals with subtracting 1 and 2 – introduces subtracting all of a set of 0.	96–100	
	● **Facts to 5:** – introduces the subtraction facts $5 - 4$, $5 - 3$, $4 - 3$ – involves counting back in ones on a number line/strip – begins to systematise subtraction facts to 5.	101–107	

	● **Subtraction language:**
	– involves subtraction word problems
	– involves alternative forms of subtraction language,
	  for example:
	  – *2 less than 4*
	  – *take 3 from 5*
	  – *subtract 1 from 3*
	– links addition and subtraction facts for 3, 4 and 5.
		108–115	

Money	● **Subtraction within 10p/£10:** – deals with reducing prices by 1p/2p and £1/£2 – introduces subtraction within 10p/£10 using coins, then mentally.	167–170	

Weight	● **Weight:**
	– deals with direct comparison of the weights of two objects by handling and by using a two-pan balance
	– explains how to use a two-pan balance and non-standard units to:
	  – weigh objects
	  – compare the weights of objects indirectly
	– introduces language associated with weighing (heavy/light, heavier/lighter, about the same weight as, balances).
		203–207	

2D Shape	● **2D Shape:** – introduces the circle, triangle, square and rectangle – with simple properties of sides and corners – introduces the hexagon.	186–189	
Assess and review			
Numbers to 20	● **Number names:** – introduces number names eleven to twenty.	35–37	
Numbers to 20	● **Ordinal numbers:** – introduces fourth, fifth, sixth, … tenth – introduces the notation 1st, 2nd, 3rd, … 10th.	38–40	
Subtraction to 10	● **Subtraction within 10:** – deals with subtracting 1 and 2 from 6–10 – deals with zero facts for 6–10 – introduces subtraction facts associated with addition doubles – explores the remaining subtraction facts to 10.	117–161	
	● **Facts for 6 and 7:** – systematises subtraction facts for 6 and 7.	124–128	
	● **Facts for 8 and 9:** – introduces and systematises subtraction facts for 8 and 9.	129–133	
	● **Facts to 10:** – systematises subtraction facts for 10 – provides word problems and practice involving subtraction facts to 10.	134–140	
	● **Subtraction: comparison:** – introduces 'how many more?' and 'difference between'.	141–147	
	● **Linking + and − facts for 6–10:** – links addition and subtraction facts for 6, 7, 8, 9 and 10.	148–151	
	● **Subtraction facts to 10:** – introduces examples of the following types: $7 - \square = 3$ and $\square - 4 = 3$.	152–155	
Time	● **Time: telling the time:** – introduces 'o'clock' and 'half past' times on analogue and digital clocks	219–224	
Data Handling	● **Sorting, matching, relationships:** – introduces Carroll diagrams – introduces arrow diagrams to show relationships.	232–235	
Assess and review			

Framework planner

Unit	Framework Topic	Objectives: children will be taught to ...
1–4	Counting, properties of number and number sequences	• Know the number names and recite them in order to at least 20 • **Count reliably at least 20 objects**
2–4	Place value and ordering	• **Read and write numerals from 0 to at least 20** • **Order numbers to at least 20** and position them on a number track.
	Understanding + and – Mental calculation strategies (+ and –)	• Use knowledge that addition can be done in any order to do mental calculations more efficiently. For example: put the larger number first and count on in ones, including beyond 10 (e.g. 7 + 5) • Identify near doubles, using doubles already known (e.g. 6 + 5) • Begin to bridge through 10 when adding a single-digit number.
	Money and 'real life' problems Making decisions	• **Use mental strategies to solve simple problems** set in 'real life' • Recognise coins of different values. Find totals and change from up to 20p Work out how to pay an exact sum using smaller coins.
5–6	Measures, including problems	• Understand and use the vocabulary related to capacity • **Compare two capacities by direct comparison;** extend to more than two • **Suggest suitable non-standard units and measuring equipment to estimate, then measure, a capacity.**
	Shape and Space Reasoning about shapes	• Use one or more shapes to make, describe and continue repeating patterns • Fold shapes in half then make them into symmetrical patterns • Talk about things that turn. Make whole turns and half turns.
7	Assess and review	

Unit	Framework Topic	Objectives: children will be taught to ...
8	Counting, properties of number and number sequences	• Know the number names and recite them in order to at least 20 • **Describe and extend number sequences: count in tens from and back to zero**
9–11	Place value, ordering, estimating	• Begin to know what each digit in a two-digit number represents.
	Understanding + and – Mental calculation strategies (+ and –)	• Use patterns of similar calculations (e.g. 10 − 0 = 10, 10 − 1 = 9, 10 − 2 = 8 ...) • Use known number facts and place value to subtract a pair of numbers mentally within the range 0 to at least 20
12–13	Measures and time, including problems	• Understand and use the vocabulary related to time Read the time to the hour or half hour on analogue clocks • **Use mental strategies to solve simple problems** set in 'real life'
	Handling data	• Solve a given problem by sorting, classifying and organising information in simple ways, such as: using objects of pictures in a list or simple table Discuss and explain results.
14	Assess and review	

NHM Topic	NHM Section	Teaching File page	Date/Comments
Numbers to 20	● **Introduction of numbers to 100:** – extends the number sequence to 39 (and then to 100) – deals with counting in ones to 39.	44–46	
Numbers to 20	● **Introduction of numbers to 100:** – extends the number sequence to 39 – deals with counting in ones to 39.	44–46	
Addition to 10	● **Addition beyond 10:** – deals with addition of 10 and a single-digit number – introduces addition of a two-digit number and a single-digit number with totals up to 20 – introduces addition of two single-digit numbers with totals greater than 10.	82–86	
Money	● **Using the 10p coin:** – introduces the 10p coin – deals with finding amounts to 20p using 1p, 2p, 5p and 10p coins.	176–178	
Capacity	● **Capacity:** – explains how to compare capacities directly by pouring – introduces using non-standard units to measure and compare capacities – deals with estimation and selection of suitable measuring units.	208–212	
2D Shape	● **2D Shape:** – gives practice in continuing and making patterns – introduces symmetry – deals with moving forward and back, turning left and right, whole turns and half turns.	189–193	
Assess and review			

NHM Topic	NHM Section	Teaching File page	Date/Comments
Numbers to 20	● **Introduction of numbers to 100:** – extends the number sequence to 100 – deals with counting in tens to 100.	44–46	
Numbers to 20	● **Introduction of numbers to 100:** – extends the number sequence to 100 – deals with counting in tens to 100.	44–46	
Addition to 10	● **Subtraction beyond 10:** – deals with subtraction of 10 from a teens number (17 – 10) – introduces the subtraction of a single digit from 20 (20–6) – extends to the subtraction of a single digit from a teens number with and without bridging of 10 (14 – 3 = 11, 14 – 5 = 9).	158–162	
Time	● **Time: durations:** – deals with finding the time 1, 2 or 3 hours before or after given digital or analogue times – introduces finding durations in whole hours between given digital or analogue times.	225–228	
Data Handling	● **Graphs:** – deals with organising, displaying and interpreting data using simple graphs.	236–238	
Assess and review			

Appendix B: Topic planner

Unit	NHM Topic	NHM Section	Teaching File page
1–4	Numbers to 20	● **Number sequence to 20:** – extends the number sequence to 20 – deals with ordering language – the number after/before, the number(s) between – introduces counting and drawing up to 20 objects – introduces counting a number of objects within a set.	18–19 23–25
		● **Comparing and ordering numbers:** – deals with recognising the larger/smaller number in a pair – deals with recognising the largest/smallest number in a set of three – includes ordering up to five non-consecutive numbers, starting with the largest/smallest – includes finding a number 1 and 2 more/less than a given number.	26–29
		● **Even and odd numbers:** – deals with counting on and back in steps of 2 – introduces even and odd numbers – introduces counting on and back in steps of 3.	30–34
		● **Number names:** – introduces number names eleven to twenty.	35–37
		● **Ordinal numbers:** – introduces fourth, fifth, sixth, … tenth – introduces the notation 1st, 2nd, 3rd, … 10th.	38–40
5	Length	● **Length:** – introduces direct comparison of lengths using language such as longer, shorter, … longest, shortest, … – introduces the use of arbitrary and non-standard units to measure and compare lengths – deals with estimation, and selection of suitable measuring units.	195–201
6	3D Shape	● **3D Shape:** – deals with recognising and naming 3D shapes using: – 'everyday' names (cube, box, ball, cone, tube) – mathematical names (cube, cuboid, sphere, cone, cylinder) – introduces language associated with 3D shapes (rolls, slides, flat, curved, face, edge, straight, corner) – deals with language associated with position (near, beside, below, under, above).	180–184
7	Assess and review		

Unit	NHM Topic	NHM Section	Teaching File page
8–11	Addition to 10	● **Addition to 5: consolidation:** – consolidates addition facts to 5 and includes the addition of three numbers – introduces examples of the type $2 + \square = 5$ and $\square + 1 = 5$.	54–58
		● **Doubles and near doubles:** – systematically introduces 'doubles' and 'near doubles' facts for addition to 10 – deals with the development of quick random recall of these facts.	59–63
		● **Addition facts for 6 and 7:** – introduces systematically the addition facts for 6 and 7 – develops quick, random recall of these facts and all previously learned.	64–68
		● **Addition facts for 8 and 9:** – introduces systematically the addition facts for 8 and 9 – develops quick, random recall of these facts and all previously learned.	69–74
		● **Addition facts to 10:** – introduces systematically the addition facts for 10 – develops quick, random recall of all facts to 10.	75–81
		● **Addition to 10p/£10:** – deals with increasing prices by 1p/2p and £1/£2 – introduces addition to 10p/£10 using coins, then mentally.	164–166
12	Data Handling	● **Sorting, matching, relationships:** – encourages children to select their own criteria for sorting – introduces Carroll diagrams – introduces arrow diagrams to show relationships.	230–235
13	Time	● **Days of the week:** – introduces the days of the week.	214–217
14	Assess and review		

Framework Topic	Objectives: children will be taught to ...	Date/Comments
Counting, properties of number and number sequences	● Know the number names and recite them in order to at least 20, from and back to zero ● **Count reliably at least 20 objects** ● **Read and write numerals from 0 to at least 20** ● Recognise and predict from simple patterns and relationships.	
Place value and ordering	● **Understand and use the vocabulary of comparing and ordering numbers** Compare two familiar numbers, say which is more or less, and give a number which lies between them ● **Order numbers to at least 20;** and position them on a number track.	
Counting, properties of number and number sequences	● Describe and extend number sequences: count on in twos from zero, then one, and begin to recognise odd or even numbers to about 20 begin to count on in steps of 3 from zero.	
Place value and ordering	● Know the number names and recite them in order to at least 20 ● **Understand and use the vocabulary of comparing and ordering numbers,** including ordinal numbers to at least 20.	
Measures, including problems	● Understand and use the vocabulary related to length ● **Compare two lengths by direct comparison;** extend to more than two ● **Suggest suitable non-standard units and measuring equipment to estimate, then measure a length.**	
Shape and Space Reasoning about shapes	● **Use everyday language to describe features of familiar 3-D shapes,** including the cube, sphere, cylinder, cone, referring to properties such as the shape of flat faces, or the number of faces or corners… ● Make and describe models, patterns and pictures using contruction kits, everyday materials, Plasticine… Begin to relate solid shapes to pictures of them ● Investigate a general statement about familiar shapes by finding examples that satisfy it ● Use everyday language to describe position, direction and movement.	
Assess and review		

Framework Topic	Objectives: children will be taught to ...	Date/Comments
Understanding + and – Mental calculation strategies (+ and –)	● **Understand the operation of addition and use the related vocabulary** Begin to recognise that addition can be done in any order Begin to use the + and = signs to record mental calculations in a number sentence, and to recognise the use of symbols such as ☐ and △ to stand for an unknown number ● Begin to recognise that more than two numbers can be added together ● **Know by heart:** addition facts for all pairs of numbers with a total up to at least 5 addition doubles for all numbers to at least 5 (e.g. 4 + 4) ● Begin to know addition facts for all pairs of numbers with a total up to at least 10 ● Identify near doubles, using doubles already known (e.g. 6 + 5) ● Use patterns of similar calculations ● Use known number facts to add a pair of numbers mentally within the range 0 to at least 10 ● **Know by heart: all pairs of numbers with a total of 10** (e.g. 3 + 7)	
Money and 'real life' problems	● **Use mental strategies to solve simple problems** set in 'real life' ● Recognise coins of different values.	
Handling data	● Solve a given problem by sorting, classifying and organising information in simple ways, such as using objects or pictures ● Discuss and explain results.	
Measures and time, including problems	● Understand and use the vocabulary related to time Know the days of the week.	
Assess and review		

Topic planner

Unit	NHM Topic	NHM Section	Teaching File page
1–4	Subtraction to 10	● **Concept of subtraction:** – deals with the concept of subtraction – introduces the language 'take away' and the '–' symbol.	92–95
		● **Subtraction involving 1, 2 and 0:** – deals with subtracting 1 and 2 – introduces subtracting all of a set of 0.	96–100
		● **Facts to 5:** – introduces the subtraction facts 5 – 4, 5 – 3, 4 – 3 – involves counting back in ones on a number line/strip – begins to systematise subtraction facts to 5.	107–107
		● **Subtraction language:** – involves subtraction word problems – involves alternative forms of subtraction language, for example: – *2 less than 4* – *take 3 from 5* – *subtract 1 from 3* – links addition and subtraction facts for 3, 4 and 5.	108–115
5	Weight	● **Weight:** – deals with direct comparison of the weights of two objects by handling and by using a two-pan balance – explains how to use a two-pan balance and non-standard units to: – weigh objects – compare the weights of objects indirectly – introduces language associated with weighing (heavy/light, heavier/lighter, about the same weight as, balances).	203–207
6	2D Shape	● **2D Shape:** – introduces the circle, triangle, square and rectangle – deals with simple properties of sides and corners – introduces the hexagon	186–189
7	Assess and review		

Unit	NHM Topic	NHM Section	Teaching File page
8–10	Subtraction to 10	● **Subtraction within 10:** – deals with subtracting 1 and 2 from 6–10 – deals with zero facts for 6–10 – introduces subtraction facts associated with addition doubles – explores the remaining subtraction facts to 10.	117–123
		● **Facts for 6 and 7:** – systematises subtraction facts for 6 and 7.	124–128
		● **Facts for 8 and 9:** – introduces and systematises subtraction facts for 8 and 9.	129–133
		● **Facts to 10:** – systematises subtraction facts for 10 – provides word problems and practice involving subtraction facts to 10.	134–140
		● **Subtraction: comparison:** – Introduces 'how many more?' and 'difference between'.	141–147
		● **Linking + and – facts for 6–10:** – links addition and subtraction facts for 6, 7, 8, 9 and 10.	148–151
	Money	● **Subtraction facts to 10:** – introduces examples of the following types: 7 – ☐ = 3 and ☐ – 4 = 3.	152–155
		● **Subtraction within 10p/£10:** – deals with reducing prices by 1p/2p and £1/£2 – introduces subtraction within 10p/£10 using coins, then mentally.	167–170
11	Data Handling	● **Graphs:** – deals with organising, displaying and interpreting data using simple graphs.	236–238
12	Time	● **Time: telling the time:** – introduces 'o'clock' and 'half past' times on analogue and digital clocks	219–224
13	Assess and review		

Framework Topic	Objectives: children will be taught to ...	Date/Comments
Understanding + and – Mental calculation strategies (+ and –)	• **Understand the operation of subtraction (as 'take away', 'difference',** and 'how many more to make') **and use the related vocabulary** Begin to use the – and = signs to record mental calculations in a number sentence, and to recognise the use of symbols such as □ or △ to stand for an unknown number • **Know by heart:** subtraction facts for all pairs of numbers with a total up to at least 5.	
Measures, including problems	• Understand and use the vocabulary related to mass • **Compare two masses by direct comparison;** extend to more than two • **Suggest suitable non-standard units and measuring equipment to estimate, then measure a mass.**	
Shape and Space Reasoning about shapes	• **Use everyday language to describe features of familiar 2-D shapes,** including the circle, triangle, square, rectangle ..., referring to properties such as the number of corners or the number and types of sides • Make and describe models, patterns and pictures using construction kits, everyday materials and Plasticine... • Investigate a general statement about familiar shapes by finding examples that satisfy it.	
Assess and review		

Framework Topic	Objectives: children will be taught to ...	Date/Comments
Understanding + and – Mental calculation strategies (+ and –)	• **Understand the operation of subtraction and use the related vocabulary** Begin to use the – and = signs to record mental calculation in a number sentence, and to recognise the use of symbols such as □ or △ to stand for an unknown number • **Know by heart** subtraction facts for all pairs of numbers with a total up to at least 10 • Use patterns of similar calculations (e.g. 10 – 0 = 10, 10 – 1 = 9, 10 – 2 = 8 ...) • Use known number facts to subtract a pair of numbers mentally within the range 0 to at least 10	
Money and 'real life' problems	• **Use mental strategies to solve simple problems** set in 'real life'.	
Handling data	• Solve a given problem by sorting, classifying and organising information in simple ways, such as: using objects of pictures; in a list or simple table • Discuss and explain results.	
Measures and time including problems	• Understand and use the vocabulary related to time Read the time to the hour or half hour on analogue clocks.	
Assess and review		

Topic planner

Unit	NHM Topic	NHM Section	Teaching File page
1–4	Numbers to 20	● **Introduction of numbers to 100:** – extends the number sequence to 39 – deals with counting in ones to 39.	44–46
	Addition to 10	● **Addition beyond 10:** – deals with addition of 10 and a single-digit number – introduces addition of a two-digit number and a single-digit number with totals up to 20 – introduces addition of two single-digit numbers with totals greater than 10.	82–88
	Money	● **Using 1p, 2p and 5p coins:** – gives practice in using 1p, 2p and 5p coins – deals with finding totals of combinations of 1p, 2p and 5p coins – introduces selecting coins to pay the exact amount for an item.	171–175
5	Capacity	● **Capacity:** – explains how to compare capacities directly by pouring – introduces using non-standard units to measure and compare capacities – deals with estimation and selection of suitable measuring units.	208–212
6	2D Shape	● **2D Shape:** – gives practice in continuing and making patterns – introduces symmetry – deals with moving forward and back, turning left and right, whole turns and half turns.	189–193
7	Assess and review		

Unit	NHM Topic	NHM Section	Teaching File page
8–11	Numbers to 20	● **Introduction of numbers to 100:** – extends the number sequence to 100 – deals with counting in tens to 100.	46–50
	Subtraction to 10	● **Subtraction beyond 10:** – deals with subtraction of 10 from a teens number (17 – 10) – introduces the subtraction of a single digit from 20 (20 – 6) – the subtraction of a single digit from a teens number with and without bridging of 10 (14 – 3 = 11, 14 – 5 = 9).	158–162
	Money	● **Using the 10p coin:** – introduces the 10p coin – deals with finding amounts to 20p using 1p, 2p, 5p and 10p coins.	176–178
12	Time	● **Time: durations:** – deals with finding the time 1, 2 or 3 hours before or after given digital or analogue times – introduces finding durations in whole hours between given digital or analogue times.	225–228
13	Data Handling	● **Graphs:** – deals with organising, displaying and interpreting data using simple graphs.	236–238
14	Assess and review		

Framework Topic	Objectives: children will be taught to ...	Date/Comments
Counting, properties of number and number sequences	• Know the number names and recite them in order to at least 20 • **Count reliably at least 20 objects.** • Read and write numerals from 0 to at least 20	
Understanding + and − Mental calculation strategies (+ and −)	• Use knowledge that addition can be done in any order to do mental calculations more efficiently. For example: put the larger number first and count on in ones, including beyond 10 (e.g. 7 + 5) • Identify near doubles, using doubles already known (e.g. 6 + 5) • Begin to bridge through 10 when adding a single-digit number.	

Money and 'real life' problems	• Recognise coins of different values
	  Find totals and change from up to 20p
	  Work out how to pay an exact sum using smaller coins.	

Measures, including problems	• Understand and use the vocabulary related to capacity • **Compare two capacities by direct comparison;** extend to more than two • **Suggest suitable non-standard units and measuring equipment to estimate, then measure, a capacity.**	
Shape and Space Reasoning about shapes	• Use one or more shapes to make, describe and continue repeating patterns • Fold shapes in half then make them into symmetrical patterns • Talk about things that turn. Make whole turns and half turns.	
Assess and review		

Framework Topic	Objectives: children will be taught to ...	Date/Comments
Counting, properties of number and number sequences	• Know the number names and recite them in order to at least 20 • **Count reliably at least 20 objects** • Describe and extend number sequences: count in tens from and back to zero	
Place value and ordering	• **Read and write numerals from 0 to at least 20** • **Order numbers to at least 20,** and position them on a number track • Begin to know what each digit in a two-digit number represents.	
Understanding + and − Mental calculation strategies (+ and −)	• Use patterns of similar calculations (e.g. 10 − 0 = 10, 10 − 1 = 9, 10 − 2 = 8) • Use known number facts and place value to subtract a pair of numbers mentally within the range 0 to at least 20	

Money and 'real life' problems	• **Use mental strategies to solve simple problems** set in 'real life'
	• Recognise coins of different values
	  Find totals of change from up to 20p
	  Work out how to pay an exact sum by using smaller coins.	

Measures and time including problems	• Understand and use the vocabulary related to time Read the time to the hour or half hour on analogue clocks • **Use mental strategies to solve simple problems** set in 'real life'.	
Handling data	• Solve a given problem by sorting, classifying and organising information in simple ways, such as: using objects of pictures; in a list or simple table • Discuss and explain results.	
Assess and review		

Appendix C: Development charts

			Number			
Counting and place value	**Addition**	**Subtraction**	**Multiplication**	**Division**	**Money**	**Fractions**
NHM R						
Numbers to 5 – counting to 5, the sequence – writing numbers – ordering numbers **Numbers to 10** – counting to 10 – writing the numbers – ordering numbers to 10 – patterns Number names to ten	**Concept of addition** – adding 2 sets – using a partitioned set – introducing language, plus and equal signs **Adding 1 and 2** – Finding addition facts for 2, 3, 4 and 5, including zero facts	**Concept of subtraction** – introducing language – taking away 1 and 2			Language associated with buying and shopping **Coins** – introduces all the coins from 1p to £2 – sorting coins in various ways – finding coins of a particular value	
NHM 1						
Numbers to 20 Revising numbers to 10 Introducing the sequence to 20 Counting to 20 Comparing and ordering numbers to 20 Counting on and back in ones and twos Odd and even numbers Number names for eleven to twenty Ordinal names and notation 1st – 5th – 10th	**Addition to 10** Consolidating facts to 5 Systematising and memorising facts to 5 Doubles facts to 5 + 5 Introducing facts for 6 to 10 Systematising and memorising facts to 10 Adding three numbers	**Subtraction within 5** – taking away using materials – subtracting 1 and 2, all or none – system attaining facts to 5 – extending the language **Subtraction within 10** Subtracting 1, 2, and zero facts Systemising facts to 10 Introducing differences between and difference in price Linking addition and subtraction facts			Increasing prices by 1p/2p, £1/£2 Buying two or three items using 1p/£1 coins Reducing prices by 1p/2p, £1/£2 Using – 1p, 2p, 5p coins – 10p coin Lay out and counting amounts up to 20p	

Numbers to 100
- the sequence
- decades
- 100-square

Adding facts beyond 10
- adding a number to 10
- using a counting on strategy
- using know facts: 3 + 2 = 5 so 13 + 2 = 15
- introducing ten-frame for bridging ten.

Subtraction beyond 10
subtracting
- 10 from a teens number
- a single digit from 20
- a single digit from a teens number
- bridging 10

NHM 2

Numbers to 100
- the sequence to 100
- introducing place value
- comparing and ordering
- counting in twos, threes, fours, fives
- number between, estimating and rounding

Numbers to 1000
- the sequence to 1000
- comparing and ordering to 999

Addition to 20
- facts to 10
- mental strategies
- facts to 15
- facts to 20

Addition to 100
- single digit to a two-digit number
- multiple of 10 to a two-digit number
- single digit with bridging
- teens number to a two-digit number; addition of three numbers

Numbers within 20
- facts to 10
- single digit from a teens number
- facts for 11–15
- facts for 16–20

Numbers within 100
- a single digit
- tens
- a single digit bridging 20
- tens and units
- using and applying
- with hundreds

- concept
- two times table
- facts for 10 and 5
- consolidation and money

- concept of sharing and grouping
- by 2 and halving
- by 10
- consolidation

- using 1p, 2p, 5p, 10p coins
- 20p, 50p, £1 coins
- counting collections greater than £1
- the notation £1.38

- halves and quarters of shapes
- notation 1/2, 1/4
- half and quarter of a set
- linking doubles to halves

	Shape		Measure				Data Handling
	3D	2D	Length	Weight	Capacity	Time	

NHM R

3D	2D	Length	Weight	Capacity	Time	Data Handling
Introducing – cube – cone – sphere – cylinder Recognising, sorting and naming shapes Building with the shapes Making 3D shape patterns	Introducing – circle – triangle – square – rectangle Recognising, sorting and naming shapes Making shape pictures Copying, continuing and creating 2D shape patterns Introduces one line of symmetry **Position and Movement** – language – turning	Language – long, short, tall, wide, narrow, thick, thin – direct comparison using language: longer, shorter, taller	Language – heavy, light – comparisons: heavier, lighter, about the same weight as Introduces a two-pan balance	Language – full, empty Filling to a mark Comparing by pouring	Language – before, after – ordering events – day, night, morning, afternoon Days of the week Nursery rhymes O'clock times on an analogue clock	Sorting by – colour – type – shape and size – selecting criteria Matching – one-to-one – sets with more – sets with the same number

NHM 1

3D	2D	Length	Weight	Capacity	Time	Data Handling
Recognising and naming – cubes – cuboids – cones – spheres – cylinders Developing language associated with 3D shapes Developing language of position	Recognising and naming – squares – circles – triangles – rectangles Looking at sides and corners Describing, continuing and creating patterns Position and movement Symmetry	Revising language and direct comparison Ordering three or more lengths Indirect comparison using feet and spans Measuring with cubes and sticks Choosing suitable units Estimating	Revising language Comparing directly by lifting and using a two-pan balance Using non-standard units to weigh objects Indirect comparison using non-standard units	Revising language Direct comparison by pouring Comparing using non-standard units Choosing suitable units and estimating	Revising days of the week and writing them Revising o'clock times on analogue clocks and introducing digital displays Half past on analogue and digital displays Simple durations in whole hours from o'clock or half past times	Sorting into sets Selecting criteria for sorting Introducing Carroll diagrams Introducing arrow diagrams to show relationships Simple bar graphs – interpreting – organising and displaying

NHM 2

Shape	Length	Weight	Volume	Time	Data handling
– consolidates recognition and naming 3D shapes – introduces the pyramid – explores properties such as faces, edges and corners – consolidates recognition and naming 2D shapes and simple properties – introduces pentagons and octagons and simple properties of sides and corners – develops shape patterns – deals with clockwise, anticlockwise and introduces the right angle – develops line symmetry	– revises non-standard units – introduces the metre – introduces the centimetre and a centimetre ruler – introduces measuring to the nearest mark	– revises non-standard units to compare weights – introduces the kilogram and the half kilogram – introduces dish scales to weigh in kilograms	– revises the use of non-standard units – introduces the litre – encourages estimation of capacities in litres – includes simple calculations involving litres	– introduces months of the year – revises o'clock and half past times on both analogue and digital displays – introduces 'quarter past' and 'quarter to' on analogue and digital displays – deals with durations of 1, 2 or 3 hours, 30 or 15 minutes	– extends earlier work on bar graphs – introduces Carroll diagrams with 2 and 4 sets – introduces Venn diagrams

Appendix D: Assessment record grid

Year: ☐ Class: ☐

Names	Numbers to 20					Addition to 10					Subtraction to 10					Activity Book						Round-up 1	Round-up 2
	Check-up 1	Check-up 2	Check-up 3	Check-up 4	Check-up 5	Check-up 6	Check-up 7	Check-up 8	Check-up 9	Check-up 10	Check-up 11	Check-up 12	Check-up 13	Check-up 14	Check-up 15	Numbers to 20	Addition to 10	Subtraction to 5	Subtraction to 10	Money		

Appendix E: Key objectives class assessment grid

Year: _____ **Class:** _____

Names

National Numeracy Strategy Key Objectives													
Count reliably at least 20 objects													
Count on and back in ones from any small number, and in tens from and back to zero													
Read, write and order numbers from 0 to at least 20; understand and use the vocabulary of comparing and ordering these numbers													
Within the range 0 to 30 say the number that is 1 or 10 more or less than any given number													
Understand the operation of addition, and of subtraction (as 'take away' or 'difference') and use the related vocabulary													
Know by heart all pairs of numbers with a total of 10													
Use mental strategies to solve simple problems using counting, addition, subtraction, doubling and halving, explaining methods and reasoning orally													
Compare two lengths, masses or capacities by direct comparison													
Suggest suitable standard or uniform non-standard units and measuring equipment to estimate, then measure a length, mass or capacity													
Use everyday language to describe features of familiar 3-D and 2-D shapes.													

Appendix F: Record of work grids

Record of work: NHM 1

Name: [   ] Year: [   ] Class: [   ]

Numbers to 20

| Number sequence to 20 | AB 1 | AB 2 | AB 3 | AB 4 | AB 5 | AB 6 | | HA 1 | CU 1 |

| Counting to 20 | PS 1 | AB 7 | AB 8 | AB 9 | PS 2 | AB 10 | HA 2 |

| Comparing and ordering numbers | PS 3 | PS 4 | AB 11 | AB 12 | PS 5 | AB 13 | HA 3 | AB 14 | HA 4 | CU 2 |

| Even and odd numbers | PS 6 | PS 7 | AB 15 | PS 6 | PS 7 | AB 16 | PS 6 | AB 17 | HA 5 | CU 3 |

| Number names | AB 18 | AB 19 | AB 20 | HA 6 |

| Ordinal numbers | AB 21 | AB 22 | CU 4 |

| Assessment | AB 23 | AB 24 | AB 25 |

| Introduction of numbers to 100 | PS 8 | AB 26 | AB 27 | PS 9 | AB 28 | AB 29 | AB 30 | AB 31 | CU 5 |

Addition to 10

| Addition to 5: consolidation | AB 1 | AB 2 | AB 3 | AB 4 | HA 7 | CU 6 |

| Doubles and near doubles | PS 10 | AB 5 | PS 11 | AB 6 |

| Addition facts for 6 and 7 | PS 12 | PS 14 | AB 7 | AB 8 | HA 8 | PS 13 | PS 14 | AB 9 | AB 10 | CU 7 |

| Addition facts for 8 and 9 | PS 14 | AB 11 | AB 12 | HA 9 | PS 14 | PS 15 | AB 13 | AB 14 | CU 8 |

| Addition facts to 10 | PS 16 | AB 15 | AB 16 | AB 17 | AB 18 | HA 10 | CU 9 |

| Assessment | AB 19 | AB 20 |

| Addition beyond 10 | PS 17 | AB 21 | AB 22 | AB 23 | CU 10 |

New Heinemann Maths 1 © SPMG 1999

Record of work: NHM 1

Name: [   ] Year: [ ] Class: [ ]

Subtraction to 10

Concept of subtraction
AB 1	PS 18	AB 2

Subtraction involving 1, 2 and 0
AB 3	HA 11	AB 4

Subtraction facts to 5
AB 5	PS 19	AB 6	PS 20	AB 7	HA 12

Subtraction language
AB 8	HA 13	AB 9	AB 10	HA 14	AB 11	CU 11

Assessment
AB 12

Subtraction within 10
AB 13	HA 15	AB 14	AB 15	PS 21	AB 16	AB 17

Facts for 6 and 7
AB 18	HA 16	AB 19	AB 20	HA 17

Facts for 8 and 9
AB 21	AB 22	HA 18	CU 12	AB 23	AB 24	HA 19

Facts for 10
AB 25	AB 26	PS 22	HA 20	HA 21	AB 27	PS 23	CU 13

Subtraction: comparison
AB 28	AB 29	HA 22	PS 24	AB 30	PS 25

Linking + and – facts for 6 to 10
AB 31	AB 32	PS 26	PS 27	HA 23

Subtraction to 10
AB 33	AB 34	CU 14

Assessment
AB 35	AB 36

Subtraction beyond 10
AB 37	AB 38	PS 28	AB 39	PS 29	CU 18

Record of work: NHM 1

Name: [ ]   Year: [ ]   Class: [ ]

Money

Addition to 10p/£10

AB 1	PS 30	PS 31	AB 2	AB 3

Subtraction within 10p/£10

AB 4	AB 5	AB 6

Using 1p, 2p and 5p coins

PS 32	PS 33	PS 34	AB 7	AB 8	AB 9	AB 10	HA 24

Assessment

AB 11	AB 12

Using the 10p coin

AB 13	AB 14	AB 15

Shape

3D Shape

PS 35	PS 36	AB 1	AB 2

2D Shape

PS 37	AB 3	AB 4	AB 5	AB 6

Measure

Length

AB 7	AB 8	AB 9	AB 10	AB 11	AB 12	AB 13

Weight

AB 14	AB 15	AB 16

Capacity

AB 17	AB 18	AB 19	AB 20

Time: days of the week

AB 21	AB 22

Time: telling the time

PS 38	PS 39	AB 23	AB 24	PS 39	AB 25	AB 26	HA 25

Time: durations

PS 40	AB 27	PS 41	AB 28	AB 29

Data Handling

Sorting, matching, relationships

PS 42	PS 43	PS 44	AB 30	PS 45	AB 31	AB 32	PS 46	AB 33	PS 47

Bar graphs

PS 48	AB 34	AB 35	PS 49	AB 36	AB 37	AB 38	AB 39

Round-up 1

1	2	3	4	5	6	7	8	9	10	11	12	13	14	15

Round-up 2

1	2	3	4	5	6	7	8	9	10	11	12	13	14	15